AN ANTHOLOGY OF ESSAYS ON VEDANTA

INDIC ACADEMY

ISBN 979-8-89133-442-7

AN ANTHOLOGY OF ESSAYS ON VEDANTA

PROF. V. KRISHNAMURTHY

INDICACADEMY

Explanation of cover design

The crux of the book is the essay titled 'VEDANATA SOPANAM', being the eighth essay in Part 1. Sopanam means staircase. These 27 shlokas of the Sopanam comprising this vedanta sopanam take you spiritually up all the way, gradually, by stages related to and graded by your ages 20 or 40 or 60 or 80.

Contents

Some Abbreviations That Have Been Used

B.G.	**Bhagavad-Gita**
Br. S.	**Brahma sutra**
I.U	**Ishopanishad**
Katha.U.	**Kathopanishad**
K.U.	**Kenopanishad**
M.U.	**Mandukyopanishad**
M.N.U.	**Mahanarayanopanishad**
Mu.U.	**Mundakopanishad**
V.S.	**Vishnu sahasranamam**

Preface

This book originally started with the essay on Vedanta Sopanam with its 27 shlokas, now the eighth essay in Part I. The other seven essays were added later to complete the basic elements of Vedanta. Hari Kiranji kindly recalled to me my contribution on my facebook of forty summaries of speeches delivered in the Global Festival of Oneness in 2021 by various experts and he got for me those summaries of mine preserved by Indica, to be included in this Anthology.

V. Krishnamurthy

Acknowledgements

This book originally started with 'Vedanta-sopanam' as a single book. It was Kiranji who suggested that several essays of mine should be added so that the book becomes a substantial contribution to Vedanta. Hence the present version IN Part I in the form of eight essays. In Part 2 I have several short essays which are summaries of lectures online given by experts in the Global Festival of 2021.

In this rewriting and formating I had yeoman help for the knitty-gritties of using Microsoft word and I am indebted to Sri R. Narayanan for all the help. I am thankful to Kiranji as well as my son Ravi who has been sponsoring several of my books along with this.

V. Krishnamurthy

Part 1

Bits of Read Wisdom

The eight essays below were written only recently. But the seeds of this knowledge were sown by my father Brahma Sri R Visvanatha Sastrigal (1882-1956). It was from him that I learnt the essentials of Vedanta, not by means of any regular teaching, but by listening to many of his lectures by him during the years 1936 to 1956.

I also asked him questions now and then on Vedantic statements and I certainly got replies, though many of his answers remained an enigma for a long time until I began to read further.

Idol Worship

Idol worship has been the hallmark of the good-old Sanatana dharma for so long that we don't know how long. But the English words 'idol worship' form an unfortunate bad translation of the word *'devatA pUjA'* which is what must have been translated as 'idol worship' by the foreigners. 'devata' is a deity invoked by proper mantras which are as old as Sanatana dharma. It is the mantra which gives the so-called 'idol' the deity status. It is the infinite quantum of mantras that are etched in the hearts of people that make Sanatana-dharma what it is.

An idol serves the same purpose for a religious devotee as a flag does for the army. Hinduism clearly lays down that mental worship is superior to the worship of images. In fact, however, it must be admitted that all worship is idol worship. Primitive man makes a scrawl of a head on wall and calls it God. Civilized man shuts his eyes and imagines an anthropo-morphic image with arms and legs and calls it God. Both are idols. The difference is not one of kind but only of degree. Hinduism has the courage to say so. It also has the humanity to admit within its fold even those who cannot rise above grossly concrete representations of God. A common illiterate labourer and an intellectual scholar require different concepts of God to satisfy them. So Hinduism declares that each can worship God in whatever form that suits his competence and stage of spiritual evolution.

The example, however, of the army flag that was given above is only an incomplete example. The idol for a religious devotee is more than a flag. The incompleteness arises as follows. Since the common mind of man cannot comprehend the abstractness and transcendence of the nameless and formless version of God, different idols and images enter the picture. Though these myriad images and idols may appear to be only symbols each of them points to the Supreme Power inherent in everybody and it is that One God who is worshipped in the form of idols and images. We are worshipping God in the idol and not the idol as God. This fundamental point in the practice of idol worship is the most important lesson to be learnt about Hinduism. So long as you think it is an idol you have not got it. People who do not believe in God propose excuses to find fault with the worship of God through idols and appear to be 'more loyal' than the religious, by putting forth the argument that God is formless and so should not be worshipped through idols. God can take any form and so the form of the idol is good enough for us to worship God.

A naïve example which goes back to Swami Vivekananda carries home this concept in a dramatic fashion. Suppose you decide to worship 'Electricity'! How will you do it? How will you represent 'Electricity'? It has no form. But then how do you bring it to view? Does it not make sense to re-present 'the God of Electricity' in the form of a glowing bulb? Here the bulb or the glow of it is all Matter. But what makes the bulb glow is the Electricity behind it. And that is exactly what we do in Idol Worship!

Here a subtle point has to be noted. The above analogy, though on the face of it rather naïve, is full of significance. Carrying the analogy further, suppose one is worshipping 'Electricity' through the form of a bulb, which cannot glow because it has fused. Would he not be laughed at? In order to make sense that 'Electricity' is behind what we are worshipping, one would look for a glowing bulb rather than a dead bulb. This is exactly the reason why we invoke the Almighty through mantras in the so-called idol worship.

QUESTION: Is the idol or icon of a deity itself the deity?

The deity is not just an idol or icon; it is that which has been invoked by mantras in the image. An idol, by constant worship through Mantras culled from the scriptures, becomes actually the very deity which has been invoked into the physical frame, by Mantra-chanting.

QUESTION: A flag is just a symbol for the nation; it is not the Nation. Does it not mean then that an idol of a deity is also only a representation and not the 'real thing'? But the Hindu tradition of giving absolute sanctity to temples and icons seems to point to the view that the icons themselves are the deities.

The answer to this question has to be carefully absorbed. In Hinduism the same question may have different answers to different levels of questioners. From the point of view that there is only one absolute Truth and everything else is only a manifestation of that Truth, an icon is only a representation and not the 'real thing'. But from the point of view of a devotee who needs to worship Divinity in name and form, the images and icons which have been sanctified by the various mantras and rituals are themselves the deities that have as much power as the Absolute. So a Balaji in Tirupati, a Nataraja in Chidambaram, a Meenakshi in Madurai, a Visvesvara-linga in Kasi, a Jagannath in Puri, a Guruvayoorappan in Guruvayyor, a Krishna in Udupi, a Varadaraja in Kanchi and a Venkatesvara in Pittsburg and hosts of such sanctified 'images and idols' should not be cast into the role of just a 'representation' of the Absolute as a flag for the army. It is with this orientation that every devotee approaches a temple and worships the deity in the temple. In the beginning his attitude is to assume that the Lord God is in the idol. But the Lord is certainly everywhere and so, in due time, the devotee, by the Lord's Grace, realises that his assumption that the Lord God is in the idol, is actually a truism. Thus what starts as an attitude or assumption, even though one may not have a belief, results in the realisation of the truth and this is far more than just belief or faith. This is the esoteric significance of idol worship. The millions of devotees who have benefited by such worship over the centuries both in their personal homes and in public temples constitute the unique testimony for the validity of this significance. The flag example is only an incomplete example.

Any worship for that matter introduces a duality between the worshipper and the worshipped and so is a comedown from the unique mental cognition of the Divinity inherent in oneself. Hinduism is therefore human enough to admit within its fold even those ordinary mortals who cannot mature, in their understanding, above the grossly concrete representations of God. In fact the religion goes even one step further. It says, in essence, each individual can worship God in whatever form that suits his competence, taste, and stage of spiritual evolution. This principle is indeed a concession to the weakness of Man. If the grossest manifestation is the only thing that suits one's taste, mood, psychological make-up or intellect, one is free to worship God in that form. Even the same person may worship an idol at one time and at another time may meditate and attempt to merge in the transcendental Reality which is the basic chip that we are all made of, if we care to look within ourselves. One may choose one's favourite deity (*ishTa-devatA*) and worship that as if it were the Ultimate. To be free to find expression to one's search for a personal God and seek His Grace for the purification of one's mind is a prerogative which every Hindu enjoys. This, in passing, is the reason why the definition of a Hindu cannot be pigeon-holed into any grid that the western mind is familiar with. It is an extension of this thought that makes Hinduism a very tolerant religion. It is this train of thought in the Hindu mind that makes it accept different Puranas extolling different deities. The Shiva Purana may say that Shiva is the greatest God, every other God is subordinate to it. The Vishnu Purana may say the same thing of Vishnu. There is no contradiction meant, implied or slurred over. Such is the eclecticism of the religion. Here we certainly invite the criticism that Hinduism is too tolerant. But, is there something like too rich a man or too beautiful a woman?

The One Being whom the sages call by many names is referred to in the neuter gender, signifying divine existence and not a divine individual. Hinduism is neither Monotheism, which contemplates the Divine in heaven nor is it polytheism which contemplates the Divine in the universe. Max Muller coined the word henotheism for indicating this tendency of the vedic seers to magnify the importance of the particular deity they are praising in a hymn at the expense of the other gods. This is a remarkable feature of Hinduism. When they say that all Gods are nothing but names and forms of the same Ultimate Transcendental Reality, they mean it. If we understand it the wrong way, we are the one to blame, not Hinduism. This is why all good explanations and presentations have to begin from the philosophical end. Naïve explanations of Hinduism without touching the basic philosophy inherent in everything in Hinduism not only do not give the truth but they run the risk of misrepresenting the religion. The strength of Hinduism, writes Monier-Williams,

lies in its infinite adaptability to the infinite diversity of human character and human tendencies. It has its highly spiritual and abstract side suited to the philosopher, its practical and concrete side congenial to the man of the world, its aesthetic and ceremonial side attuned to the man of the poetic feeling and imagination and its quiescent contemplative aspect that has its appeal for the man of peace and the lover of seclusion.

The Absolute Brahman, in relation to the material universe, is called ISvara. When we refer to ISvara in His creative aspect, we call Him BrahmA; when we refer to His aspect of sustainer and protector, we call Him Vishnu; and when we think of Him in His destructive and dissolutive aspect, we refer to Him as Shiva. In each case the power or energy of the aspect is referred to as the corresponding Goddess. Just as sunlight is inseparable from the sun, so also is the power *(shakti)* of Ishvara inseparable from Ishvara and India naturally worships this power as Shakti, the Mother of the Universe.

QUESTION: But the practice of deity worship through idols and images seems to throw to the winds the majestic concept of Impersonality so emphatically asserted in the Upanishads. How can this be explained?

It must be admitted that all worship is image worship. Primitive man made a scrawl of a head on a rock and called it God. Civilized man shuts his eyes and imagines an anthropomorphic image with arms and legs and calls it God. Both are images. The difference is not one of kind but of degree. Hinduism has the courage to say so and also has the humanity to admit within its fold even those who cannot rise above grossly concrete representations of God. An illiterate commoner and an intellectual scholar require different concepts of God or Divinity to satisfy them. So Hinduism declares that each can worship Divinity in whatever form that suits the competence and stage of spiritual evolution of the worshipper.

TIP of the Iceberg – Transcendence, Immanence and Perfection

How to describe God? Words cannot express Him. The eyes cannot see Him. The ears cannot hear Him. He cannot be indicated as this or that. He cannot be related to something as subject and object. He is taller than the tallest. He is shorter than the shortest. There is nothing greater; nothing smaller. He cannot be predicated as the doer of some action, because the undoing of that action is also His. He cannot be attributed as the possessor of something because He possesses also the opposite of that something. He cannot be thought of by the mind, because He is not the *object* of any thought-process. He cannot be gender-specified, therefore to call Him as a 'He' itself is a failure of words. For all you know 'He' can be a 'She'! So the Upanishad*s* also refer to Him as IT. It is incomprehensible, unfettered, uncontaminated, unattached. It has no before, no after, no middle, no inner, no outer. It cannot be classified by category or by action or by quality or by relation. Because He thus transcends everything and also includes everything, He is called Vishnu which means He who overlaps everything that can be conceived. He is beyond everything. He is beyond time, beyond space, beyond causation. He is the grandest, ever. He is the supreme-most. He is therefore *purushottama* — which literally means the SUPREME PERSON. But here, 'person' does not simply mean a person in the ordinary sense of the word. The supremeness indicates that any *personification is itself transcended.* It indicates complete transcendence of everything. Our finite expressions can never do justice to the grandeur that is God. He is the Colossus, as it were, spanning everything. This is the **TRANSCENDENCE** aspect of God

He is immanent in everything. There is nothing in which He is not there. Whatever we see, whatever we hear. whatever we smell, whatever we touch, whatever we feel, is all full of that Divinity, that is He. The universe that is visible and can be also mentally visualised is the concrete expression of that self-luminous spirit that is He. He is therefore *viSvaM*, the Universe itself. Without Him there is nothing that exists. He is the substratum behind everything that is inanimate. He is the soul of everything that is animate. While He is infinitely higher than ourselves, He is also infinitely near to us. He is nearer to us than our hands and feet and mind. He is the soul of our souls. He is the Ultimate Reality behind everything that is tangible either to the senses or the mind. He is the Cause of every effect and so He is the Cause of all Causes. Not only does the Universe spring from Him but ultimately it dissolves in Him. So He is both the effective cause and the material cause. The nearest expression in 'name' and 'form' for this Immanent Absolute is the Siva-*linga* which represents the Ultimate when the entire universe has merged into it. He is the One that survives in us from childhood to adulthood and through old age from birth, as the I that we talk of when we refer to ourselves. He dwells in us as the only permanent resident. He is the real, the inner 'I". This 'I' never changes. If we write out all that might be called 'mine', including one's physical possessions, one's relatives, one's own body and limbs, mind, mental opinions, all that can be classified as 'my...' and throw out all this, then what remains is "I". This 'I' is the self of the upanishads. It is that which we see beyond right and wrong, beyond effect and cause, beyond past and future. He is the soul of our very understanding though we may not understand Him. He is Consciousness itself. He controls our very intellect from within. He is the inner controller. He is the *antar-AtmA* of everything. This is the **IMMANENCE** aspect of God.

He is perfect. He is so perfect that we may not be able to visualise the perfection. This perfection, both in action and in peace, is symbolised by the Siva-*naTarAja* icon in its famous dancing form. But God descends from this pedestal of perfection and assumes an imperfection in terms of a name and form so that we mortals may be guided from our extremities of imperfection onto the path towards perfection. This descent of the Divine from its divine pedestal is called an Avatara. The complete such Avatara is supposed to be Krishna. But in this Avatara God's mystic powers of *tirodhAna* (= illusion, deception) have been so much interwoven with His other functions that, for us, it is difficult to understand the perfection in Him. Maybe that is why the Avatara as Rama has been extolled as the model of perfection for us humans to follow and emulate. He is an *AdarSa-purusha* (Model for Emulation). In fact he is called a *suvrata* — one who has the best vows, the best character, the best behaviour. The word *vrata*, in Sanskrit, indicates a fundamental way of life from which one does not swerve. That His *vrata* is great, good, unexcelled, is what *suvrata* says. Rama's *vrata* was five-fold: To give protection to all those who sought his refuge; to abide strictly by the promised words of the father and mother; to be responsible, as a king, to the people of his kingdom even at the cost of his own personal comfort; to be totally unperturbed in the most adverse of circumstances; and never to flaunt his real (divine) stature which was always hidden behind his human exterior. This five-fold *vrata* was so excellently and so exemplarily pursued by him throughout his life that even after several millenia, his very name itself is Divinity personified in the entire Hindu world. This is the PERFECTION aspect of God.

T*ranscendence*, I*mmanence* and P*erfection* constitute only the **TIP** of the iceberg, that is God! Here are just a few sample quotes from the Scriptures

यो विज्ञाने तिष्ठन् विज्ञानाद् अन्तरः
यम् विज्ञानम् न वेद यस्य विज्ञानम् शरीरं
यो विज्ञानम् अन्तरो यमयति
एष आत्मा अन्तर्याम्य्-अमृतः ।

yo vijnAne tishTan, vijnAnAd antaraH,
yam vijnAnam na veda, yasya vijnAnam
SarIraM, yo vijnAnam antaro yamayati
esha AtmA antaryAmy-amritaH.

— Br.U.III-7-22

He who dwells in the understanding, yet is within the understanding, whom the understanding does not know, but whose body the understanding is, who controls the understanding from within, He is your self, the Inner Ruler, the Immortal.

AaN allan; peN allan; alla aliyum allan;
KANalum allan; uLan allan; illai allan;
PENungal, pENum uru Ahum; allanum Am;
kOnai peridu udaittu em pemmanaik
kurudalE.

— Tiru-vai-mozhi (Tamil)

Neither male, nor female, nor sexless;

Nor visible to the senses; neither being, nor non-being;

He has that form you desire; He is also formless;

Impossible it is to describe our Lord.

paRRudal anRi undo adaikkalam pakarkinRAnai.

— Kamba-Ramayanam, Yuddha Kandam:410

He who has come to me as refuge, how can I do anything other than taking him?

adaindavarkku aruLAn Ayin aRam en Am ANmai en Am.

— Kamba-Ramayanam, Yuddha Kandam:413

If we do not give refuge to those who seek refuge, what to speak of Dharma, what of manliness?

Mama paN SaraNAgat bhayahAri.

— Ramcharitmanas: Sundarkand: 4 (Hindi)

My vow is to take away the fear out of those who take refuge in me.

sakRd-eva prapannAya tava asmi iti cha yAchate; abhayam sarva-bhutebyo dadAmyetad-vratam mama.

— Valmiki Ramayanam.VI-18-33

Whatever being comes to me even for once and says he is mine, I give him protection and this is my *vrata* for life.

The Non-Absolutist School

The seeds of the concept of bhakti (= devotion; spiritual love) go back to even the vedas. The plant of bhakti sprouts in the Upanishads; becomes a full-fledged plant in the *itihAsas,* particularly the mahA-bhArata, blossoms in the purANas, and flowers in the *Agamas* both of the Saivite and vaishNavite varieties. The AlvArs and nAyanmArs bring out the fruits which ripen in the age of the AcAryas for all posterity to consume, enjoy and attain beatitude. The personal God with all His superlative attributes is worshipped mainly in six forms – Siva, Vishnu, Shakti, SUrya, GaNapati and SubrahmaNya.

Among the various non-Absolutist conceptions of God **Sri Ramanuja's** is the most well known, has the largest following and has the claim to the longest tradition. It conceives of a Personal God with infinite divine attributes and infinite varieties of auspicious forms. He, however, is the single Conscious Entity that has all matter and all the souls as His body. He has infinite compassion for the souls and so He is greatly concerned about their salvation. The soul has to comprehend this Inner Reality, rid itself of the three-fold miseries of life and merge in the infinite bliss of the eternal sanctity of God. This is moksha. This is a communion with God, not a realization of complete identity. Those who desire this, should practise a seven-fold discipline – namely,

1. The discretion of consuming only the right type of pure food;
2. Dispassion;
3. The attitude of living in the presence of the Absolute;
4. The action of the five daily rituals *(yajnas)*,
5. The ethics of a dhArmic life,
6. Absence of frustration and, finally,
7. The absence of delusion caused by affluence and material happiness.

Such a one does his duties as the dictates of the Lord and in total dedication to Him. This leads first to internal purity and in due time blesses one with the insight of Yoga wherein one can visualise the Spirit. That leads to the awareness of the Soul of all Souls. Love of God pours forth spontaneously now. It is a self-forgetting Love that continues uninterruptedly like the pouring out of oil. This is the bhakti. The Lord may be conceived of as your guide, your master, your friend, your child, your beloved. Each one of these perfects the devotional attitude and ends up by creating the irresistible urge to see Him in person. That is the stage of bhakti par excellence. And when that vision of the Supreme Person sparks then is the stage of Supreme Enlightenment. Thereafter there is no return to the mundane living. The Lord then frees you from the bodily prison and takes you to His abode to live in fellowship with Him.. The thing that makes this happen is only the Grace of the Lord and nothing else. That is why the Lord is said to be both the ultimate goal (upeyaM) as well as the path (upAya) to that goal. Such a faith ends up in the action of surrender to the Lord. Desika lists eight kinds of devotion which epitomise the concept of spiritual love in a masterly fashion:

1. Feeling at home in the company of devotees;
2. Enjoying the worship of the Lord;

3. An unsatiated eagerness to listen to the stories of God;
4. Horripilation and choking of voice when hearing about Him, talking to Him and remembering Him;
5. Performing of ritual pujA to the deities;
6. Not showing off in one's service to God;
7. Meditation of Him and Him only; and
8. Praying to Him, never for mundane trivialities.

Nimbarka of the twelfth century propagated what is called *dvait Adaita* school of thinking; dvaita is duality and advaita is non-duality. According to Nimbarka the souls and the universe are different from the Absolute which rules them. Yet just as the spider's web though different from the spider which has woven it is still one with the spider because it is nothing but the saliva of the spider it is the Lord that has become the souls and the universe. Thus difference and non-difference are emphasized equally. Difference is when existence is separate though not independent. Non-difference is the impossibility of separate existence. Like the ocean and the waves, like the Sun and its Light, there is difference and at the same time non-difference. One should take the

Absolute brahman as the Soul of all souls and of the Universe, comprehend this difference-in-non-difference and surrender oneself to the Lord in toto. The attitude of Radha to Krishna is what is recommended by this school. SrImad BhAgavatam is the most respected scripture.

To the great **Madhwa-AcArya** (13th century) is to be attributed the credit for the massive propagation of the school of duality (dvaita). Lord Vishnu with all his attributes and forms is the Absolute Truth and God Almighty. He has a tremendous compassion towards his creation. He gives men what they deserve according to their past karma and their present tendencies. He is the protector of every soul. The three concepts *cit, acit and ISvara* are all three different. Lord Vishnu creates by his Will. Those who desire mokSa should start from the hypothesis of God being the master and man his servant and live his life by serving Him and dwelling on the glories of God. This would generate the right bhakti in him. By doing God's will, one nurtures this bhakti. Finally by His Grace one attains salvation and experiences the state of Bliss in proportion to the sAtvic deeds he has done. The goal of life is to serve God both in this life and in the after-life. The role model of this bhakti is Hanuman of the Ramayana. The entire philosophy of bhakti of this school is enjoyably summarised in a mini-encyclopaedic work - *hari-kathA-mRta-sAram* - of Jagannatha-dasa of the eighteenth century. That the Lord is such a compassionate One who takes ten steps towards you the moment you take one step towards Him is an accepted maxim of all schools of philosophy. But the dramatic and figurative way in which Jagannatha-dasa expresses this is inimitable. Says he: 'The Lord is always one step ahead. If the devotee prays from a reclining position, God sits and listens. If the devotee appeals sitting, God stands attentively. If the former stands, God walks around him and registers his requests. If he walks and prays, God displays his love by ecstatic dancing and jumping'! The conclusion of course is implied: If the devotee dances and jumps in his chanting, what will not He do for him?

VallabhAcArya of the 15th and 16th centuries spread the theory of SuddhAdvaita. According to this the glorious Krishna in His sat-chid-Ananda form is the Absolute brahman. He is permanently playing out His sport (leela) from His seat in the *goloka* which is even beyond the divine vaikunTHa, the abode of Vishnu. Creation is His sport. To obtain the Bliss given out by Krishna the only path is bhakti. But in this age of kali, the scripture-sanctioned bhakti is impossible to practise. So what is recommended is *pushhTibhakti*–which we can all get from the natural Grace of God just like that, for no reason whatsoever. It is that bhakti which gives itself up body, heart and soul to the cause of God. It is considered to be the fullest expression of what is known as Atma-nivedana (= giving-up of oneself) among the nine forms of bhakti. It is the bhakti of the devotee who worships God not for any reward or presents but for His own sake. Such a devotee goes to goloka after leaving this body and lives in eternal bliss enjoying the sports of the Lord. The classical example of this complete self-effacement is that of the cow-herdesses towards Krishna. They spoke no word except prayer and they moved no step except towards Krishna. Their supreme-most meditation was on the lotus-feet of Krishna.

Sri Krishna Chaitanya of the 16th century is universally known for his propagation, by excellent example of his own life, of the *acintya-bheda-abheda* philosophy and the conviction about the Radha-Krishna theme that popularised Radha as a Goddess and an avatAra of Lakshmi. The relationship between the Lord and His consort is that of difference within non-difference and is therefore mentally unimaginable. The Lord is having an eternal sport with Radha. By his charming sports and beautiful form He mesmerises Man, corrects him and blesses him. bhakti is the only means to reach Him. By constant practice of the instruments of bhakti, and by cultivating a taste for the names of the Lord, compassion for the living, service to the servants of God, one increases one's component of satva-guNa (=divine tendency) and his devotion now becomes a passion for the divine in due course. This leads step by step to a state of supreme ecstasy. To reach this one may start from the silent bhakti of Bhishma, move on to the vAtsalya (filial affection) bhakti of Yasoda, the friendly bhakti of Arjuna, the dAsya bhakti (devotion by a servant) of Hanuman and finally reaches the mAdhura bhakti (devotion of Love) of the gopis– where the relationship between the devotee and the Lord is that of the spouse to the beloved. This form of bhakti is most graphically portrayed in gIta-govinda of **Jayadeva** of the 12th century.

Starting from **Jnaneswar** of the 13th century, the Maharashtrian tradition brought forth a philosophy which in some sense unified the two paths of jnAna and bhakti. According to this school, the ultimate brahman is both attributeless and attributed — that is, both impersonal and personal. To reach the Personal Ultimate one needs the bhakti of Love. To reach the Formless Ultimate one needs Enlightenment. For the former there is any one of nine methods which are classical –

1. Listening to recitals of the names and glories of God *(SravaNa)* as did King ParikSit
2. Oneself reciting the names of God *(nAma-saMkIrtana)* as did Narada;
3. Recalling Him and His deeds *(smaraNa)* as did the sage Suka
4. Waiting on Him *(pAda-sevana)* as did Lakshmana
5. Worshipping Him *(arcana)* as did King Ambarisha
6. Saluting Him *(vandana)* as did Akruraand Uddhava;
7. Serving Him *(dAsya)* as did Hanuman and Garuda

8. Befriending Him *(sakhya)* as did Arjuna and Sugriva; and
9. Dedicating oneself to Him *(Atma-nivedana)* as did King Baliand Kannappar

To reach the Impersonal Ultimate one needs to discipline oneself through the three-fold ascent of *ShravaNa* (listening), *manana* (deliberation on what has been learnt) and *nididhyAsana* (the analysis and synthesis of the accrued knowledge). This school has a stronghold in the Maharashtra area because of a succession of great devotees and expositors like **Namdev** (13th and 14th centuries) **Eknath** (16th century), **Tukaram** (17th century) and **Samarth Ramdas** (also of the 17th century).

The Advaitic School and the Message of Oneness

The scriptures are innumerable; the things to be known are many; the time at our disposal is short; the obstacles are too many. It is therefore important to grasp the essence and essence only. It is in this sense that we should approach the message of one-ness taught by the Advaita school led by Sankara. The philosophy that Sankara propagated was not his own. It was already in the Upanishads. What he did was to focus his searchlight on it and prove to us that it was the central and only teaching of the Upanishads as well as their collective last word. But the ordinary layman who remembers Sankara now does not know enough about him or his philosophy to understand him well. The only thing he can say is that Sankara taught about mAyA or illusion. 'Illusion' is a wrong translation of mAyA. By translating mAyA as illusion we have done the greatest disservice to Sankara. It is not being said that the world does not exist. It is only being said that the world is an appearance, not totally real. Sankara distinguishes three orders of reality. The Absolute Reality, that is brahman and brahman alone. The complete unreality, like the horns of a hare, or like squaring the circle if one wants to use the modern scientific language. In between these two extremes there is a phenomenal reality which is like the apparent reality of the dream world. A dream is neither real nor unreal. It is real to the person who dreams. It is unreal to the same person after he wakes up from the dream. This is the most important point. A dream is not a dream or illusion to the dreamer. So long as we dream, so long as we are seeing only the plurality of this mundane world, it is as real to us as the dream is to the dreamer. The world is unreal only to the seer who has waken up to the reality of the Absolute — like a Ramana Maharishi or a SadaSiva Brahmendra. For them the only real thing is the Absolute brahman. What they see before them is also brahman. They see brahman everywhere. So the world has not vanished absolutely. The world has vanished from their point of view. So if they keep on telling you that the world is an illusion or mithyA, it is like someone appearing in your dream and telling you, you better wake up from the dream and wake up to the reality. We are so much engrossed in our dream that we are not prepared to listen to the advice of the guru or the Upanishads or to Sankara. Thus between the formless and nameless Absolute which is the Ultimate Reality and the total unreality of non-existence, there is the intermediary apparent reality of this phenomenal world — which appears to be real but is not absolutely real. This appearance of the world as a reality has been given several analogies by philosophers. **The most telling example of this is that of a rope appearing in twilight as a snake. The snake was never there. Even when the snake was being seen there was only the rope. The rope appeared as the snake. So also brahman appears to us as the world. Even when the world is being seen it is brahman that is being seen as the world. This the seers do know and so what they see is not the world but brahman**. One may object to this analogy as follows. I realise that there was no snake. So the rope no more appears to me., So also I realise that there is only brahman and there is no reality of the world. But still the world is appearing to me. For this Ramana Maharishi asks you to go the example of the mirage. The water in the mirage is only an illusion. I see the water in the mirage. I go near it and realise that there is no water. But once I come back I see there is again the appearance of the water. This analogy is to tell you that how even after realisation, the illusion may still appear as real.

Let us accept that **any analogy has its own limitation**. The analogies have to be taken only to that extent where we do not overdo it. Once the point of the analogy is made, there is no use in continuing the analogy. Thus here the objection is raised as follows. The water of the mirage does not quench my thirst, but in this supposedly unreal world, I have my thirst, hunger etc. and all these are quenched by the happenings in this world. For this Ramana asks you to look at the analogy of the dream. Within the dream you may have thirst, and it may be quenched by the water in the dream; so also hunger. Dream analogy is a great blessing. What else is a dream for? Nobody knows. In God's creation, the value of a dream seems to be only this. To tell you how unreal is the world. Without the dream analogy it is impossible even to mentally conceive of the possible unreality of the phenomenal world from a different point of view, namely the absolute point of view. A dreamer wakes up usually only when something unpleasant happens within his dream. No dreamer ends up his dream while still in the happy state, except when an external force acts. This is because man's natural state is happiness. Realising one's natural state of happiness is *moksha*, according to Sankara. By a complete absorption of the body, mind and intellect in this eternal state of knowledge and happiness is what is called realisation of one's self. **In order to do this one has not to chase it or do anything else, says Sankara. The removal of Ignorance is the only thing to be done. Automatically our natural state will be realised.**

So what are we supposed to do at all? Sankara says: Do an introspection and investigate about your self starting the probing from a ruthless analysis of your own mind and its vagaries. Try to get away from *its* external occupations and make it preoccupied with questions like; What is making the mind think? What is really behind it? Who is the thinker? Why are you not able to control the mind? What is more permanent than the mind? Wherefrom does the mind derive its strength? Besides the physical brain where the external hardware processes the thoughts of the mind, what is the software that forms the source for all the vibrations of the mind? Whence does it spring forth? Who is operating this software? If the answer comes up saying that it is *you* who are operating the software, then is that 'you' different from the 'you' which stands behind, watching the mind? Can you watch the mind unperturbed by any of its goings-on? In that sense can you still the mind? Now who is this 'you'? Sankara and all the other exponents of advaita plead with us to keep on asking these questions and try to get convincing answers within oneself from oneself. Certainly they also ask us to go to a teacher. But a teacher can only point the way. The final analysis has to be done by oneself on oneself. Seers have declared emphatically that the quality and intensity of the internal struggle to get at these answers differ from person to person and it depends upon one's stage of spiritual evolution and the struggle he has already put in through all his various lives.

The person who is already spiritually ripe because of his earlier *vAsanA*, will probably get the enlightenment just by one listening to the teaching from the guru. But for the rest of us who are still far below this stage, Sankara says: Occupy your mind with God rather than with such secular pursuits as learning the gymnastics of rules of grammar:

भज गोविन्दं भज गोविन्दं गोविन्दं भज मूढमते
संप्राप्ते सन्निहिते काले न हि न हि रक्षति डुकृञ्करणे

bhaja govindaM bhaja govindaM
govindaM bhaja mUDhamate /
saMprApte sannihite kAle na hi na hi
rakshhati DuhRRin~karaNe

Seek the company of the good. Through the company of the good, there arises non-attachment; through non-attachment, there arises freedom from delusion; through delusionlessness, there arises steadfastness; through steadfastness, there arises liberation in life:

सत्संगत्वे निस्संगत्वं निस्संगत्वे निर्मोहत्वं
निर्मोहत्वे निश्चलतत्वं निश्चलतत्वे जीवन्मुक्तिः

satsangatve nissangatvaM nissangatve
nirmohatvaM /
nirmohatve nishcalatatvaM nishcalitatve
jIvanmuktiH //

Do not be proud of wealth, kith and kin, and youth; Time takes away all these in a jiffy. Leaving aside this entire world which is transitory, and knowing the state of brahman, enter into it.

मा कुरु धन-जन-यौवन-गर्वं हरति निमेषात्-कालस्-सर्वं
माया-मयम्-इदम्-अखिलं हित्वा ब्रह्म-पदं त्वम् प्रविश विदित्वा

mA kuru dhana-jana-yauvana-garvaM
harati nimeshAt-kAlas-sarvaM /
mAyA-mayam-idam-akhilaM hitvA
brahma-padaM tvam pravisha viditvA //

Sing the song of the Gita. Recite and revel in the one thousand names of Vishnu. Meditate on the form of the Goddess. Take the mind into the company of the good. Distribute wealth among the needy. Be devoted completed to the lotus-feet of the Master. Then, through the discipline of the mind and the control of the senses you can behold the Absolute who resides in your heart. Make no difference between the God Absolute and the Master to whom you have surrendered. Even matters that have not been explicitly declared in the scriptures will become manifest to such a seeker.

So it all comes down to Devotion to the Absolute, or devotion to the guru who is nothing but the Absolute. In such a devotion, there is to be no distinction between God and God. The usual talk among the masses about the worship of Siva or Vishnu (the two major Gods of the Hindu trinity) being two contrary disciplines does not make sense to Sankara. There is not only no difference; they are one and the same. The Absolute in two garbs, that is all. Sankara is so convinced about the importance of this non-difference that he prays to God in one of his *stotras*, as if he were afraid that he himself might get lost and lose his conviction in this maze of confusion prevalent in this world!: Oh Goddess Ganga! When it is time to lay off my body on the banks of your sacred waters, happily meditating on the lotus-feet of *nArAyaNa*, may the unqualified devotion to the everlasting one-ness of *hari* and *hara*, the non-dual Supreme, become the blessed festivity in me of bidding good-bye to this life.! Here and elsewhere, *hari* and *hara* are alternate names for Vishnu and Siva respectively. The first step in understanding the non-dual philosophy of Sankara is this non-difference of Siva and Vishnu. The next step is to realise that this one God is not only transcendent but also immanent in every one of the living beings. This makes Sankara define devotion as nothing but the contemplation of one's real self.:

स्वस्वरूपानुसन्धानं भक्तिरित्यभिधीयते

svasvarUpA-nusandhAnaM
bhaktir-ity-abhidhIyate

As oil dwells in the oil-seed, as curd in milk, as water in a ground-water source or as fire in firewood so does He dwell in the Universe:

तिलेषु तैलं दधिनीव सर्पिः आपः स्रोतस्वरणीषु चाग्निः

tileSu tailaM dadhinIva sarpiH Apah
Srotas-varaNIshu cAgniH...

says *SvetASvatara-upanishad*. This Absolute is everywhere, in front of us, behind us, above us, below us, to the right of us, to the left of us – the scriptures do not tire of repeating this kind of refrain. And all this is in oneself, i.e., one's Self. This Self is everywhere. That is why the *ISa*-Upanishad says: It is already there before even the fastest mind goes there. In the entire philosophical thought process of the world this thought that the whole universe is immanent in oneself is a giant leap for mankind. When the universe dissolves in the Ultimate, it is a stepwise dissolution. From earth to water, from water to fire, from fire to air, from air to space – these are the stages of dissolution. Finally what remains is Space. Even that space finally will dissolve in the *Atman*, says the scripture. Can we imagine this situation when there is nothing, not even space? It is to help us attempt the mental gymnastics of comprehending this that all the scriptures cry hoarse on this topic.

Great devotees and exponents of the Advaitic school (of Sankara) have extolled the qualities and pleasures of *bhakti* so eloquently that for the ordinary man there should be no doubt about the fundamental role of *bhakti* in *advaita*. But critics of *advaita* as well as laymen who have not cared to take the effort to understand what *advaita* is, do sometimes declare that *bhakti* is not concordant with the concept of *advaita* and to be a devotee is not the forte of an Advaitin. Their question is: how can *bhakti* coexist with *advaita*? According to them, the teaching (of *advaita*) that the Self of each individual is the same as the Supreme Self is contradictory to the duality implied in the concept of *bhakti*. In the process of devotion there is always a duality involved - namely, the worshipper and the worshipped. If God or the Supreme Reality does not have a separate status other than our Selves, then who is to worship whom? *advaita* means non-duality. There is no second object in existence other than the Supreme Godhead. So where is the leeway for any worship or devotion? Says Sankara in his *Siva*nanda-Lahari (Verse No.81): Sometime in worshipping the lotus-feet of God, sometime in meditation and concentration, sometime in offering obeisance, sometime in listening to His stories, sometime in looking at His form, sometime in singing His praise, he who gains such a state in exhultation, having surrendered his mind to God, is verily a *Jivan-mukta*, the highest state of Spiritual Love. It is the same Sankara who declares through all his commentaries and *prakarana-granthas* that Knowledge alone — neither an integration of Knowledge and Works nor an integration of Knowledge and Devotion — that leads to *moksha.* But to get to that state of Knowledge where one perceives nothing else, because there is only the Perceiver, he strongly recommends the doing of Works in a desireless unattached way and with a one-pointed devotion to the Ultimate. In order to impress upon us laymen that this is the only way to ascend to spiritual heights, he tours the whole country more than once, visits almost every important temple and place of pilgrimage and sings his compositions in praise of the revered deities of that place in the most eloquent poetry. He it is who has established the tradition of ritually worshipping together all the five divinities – *sUrya*, the Sun-God; *Sakti*, the Mother; Vishnu, *gaNeSa* and Siva — of the Hindu tradition through a sophisticated ritual called the *panchAyatana pUja*, meaning worship at five altars. Here the divinities are worshipped not in their human-like forms but in certain symbols in the form of stones, which are nothing but certain rock formations available in specified locations in the country. **This tradition may be taken as an intermediate stage between the worship of Godhead with form and the worship of the formless, because the symbols of worship as rock formations have certainly a form but they are also formless in that they have no parts like face, eyes, body, hands or feet.** It is as though the devotee trains himself to take the mind from the forms to the formless while at the same time allowing full scope for his emotional feelings of devotion and surrender. It is because of this that invocation mantras in the advaitic tradition contain effectively the following idea as the core of the mantra. Oh God! I know you are omnipresent. But, for the purpose of my concentration and worship please condescend to make your presence felt here in this idol (image, picture or stone or whatever) for the period of the *pUjA*; maybe I am insulting your omnipresence by requesting you to confine yourself to this form and space, but please pardon me; I know no other way'.

The ascent from our physical, vital, emotional and intellectual being into the supermind of spiritual being is spiritual evolution. The technology of this ascent is Spiritual Love. There are at least three stages through which one has to rise. The first is *bAhya bhakti* or external *bhakti*. This is adoration of something outside ourselves. It is based on the unenlightened *tAmasik* feeling that God is external to us and that He dwells in a particular locality – a temple, a shrine or a holy place or bathing ghAT. Popular religion does not usually rise above this level. The second stage of *bhakti* is *ananya bhakti*, the exclusive and passionate (*rAjasik*) worship of one's favourite deity. It is in fact an intense monotheism. The entire Ram-charit-manas of Tulsidas is a monumental example of the purity and majesty of *ananya-bhakti*. The third stage of *bhakti* is *ekAnta bhakti*, the purest (*sAtvik*) form. Here the worshipper loves God for His own sake and not for His gifts, not even for *moksha*. It is free from the feeling for any other object. It is the service of the Lord – an adoring service that implies centering of the mind on Him, expecting no gain either here or hereafter. It is a constant flow of mind, brimming with love towards the Lord and His creation, without any selfish desire. All his activities are sublimated into worship of the Divine. Whatever he does, whatever he eats, whatever he offers, is all a dedication to the Divine, not just as a formality, as ordinary virtuous people profess to be doing, but in total reality. Such a devotee appears to be doing external activities but since his ego is in total sublimation to the Divine he is not doing anything for himself. Even the distinction between sacred and secular activity disappears in such a soul. Every work is sacred to him inasmuch as it is an expression of his love of God. This supreme love of God was expressed by the cowherdesses of Brindavan. Their love can be understood by us only if, in the words of Swami Vivekananda 'we can forget our love of gold, name and fame and this little material world of ours'. Their love, even though it originated in a kind of physical desire, rose up to the highest plane of self-effacing love of God, because of the holy association of the Divine, and thus in its final stages became the pinnacle of perfection of *bhakti*.

The artistic manifestation of this *bhakti* can take place in one or more of nine ways – says Prahlad, the Devotee par excellence. This statement of his occurs as a spirited reply of a boy of five years old to the arrogant father's seemingly innocent query about the former's progress in his study-in-residence with the guru. **It is one of the grandest pronouncements of the Hindu religion, that has since been quoted across the world billions of times**. And it says:

That action is the greatest lesson one learns which expresses itself in terms of the nine manifestations of devotion to Lord Vishnu, namely, Listening to recitals of the names and glories of God (*ShravaNa*), Oneself reciting the names of God (*nAma-sankIrtana),* Recalling Him and His deeds *(smaraNa),* Waiting on Him (*pAdasevana*), Worshipping Him (*arcana*),

Saluting Him (*vandana*), Serving Him (*dAsya*), Befriending Him (*sakhya*) and Dedicating oneself to Him (*Atma-nivedana*).

It is not the name of the deity, Vishnu or Narayana, that is important here. The name is not there to distinguish it from the other names of God. This is the purport of *advaita*. Whether it is Siva or Vishnu, all the references are only to the One Supreme God – this is the intent of the Vedas. 'He is Brahma, He is Siva, He is Hari, He is Indra, He is the Imperishable, He is the Transcendental Supreme' says the Narayanopanishad part of Yajur Veda. This teaching of non-difference is most important for the understanding of Hinduism - says Sankara. It is not even correct to say Sanatana Dharma - says Sankara. It is not even correct to say that Siva and Vishnu are 'equal' says the Mahaswami of Kanchi. 'They are the same; just as the same actor appears in different roles, one is the Paramatma (=Transcendental Supreme) dressed as Vishnu and the other is Paramatma dressed as Siva. Throughout the vedic literature one will find various divinities Varuna, Indra, Soma, Agni and Surya each glorified at one point to the exclusion of everything else. Any attempt to dissect the meanings and find a logical hierarchical explanation in the worldly literary sense of characters in literary fiction, would fail miserably. The entire mythological set-up embedded in the multitude of our *purANa*s, if taken at their story-value without any feeling for the under-current of the oneness of the Almighty, will create nothing but chaos in our intellectual understanding. The different hymns eulogising the different gods and goddesses are couched either in simple language with complex meanings or in complex language which perhaps hide simple ideas. It is very easy to misunderstand their significance and meanings. Western interpreters who have not got into the spirit of the religion have erred in a colossal manner. If you carefully look at the superlatives being used in the Vedic literature in the same manner and language for each Vedic deity and if you look at the exact imitations of these eulogies made by the *purANa*s for the various other manifestations of the Ultimate Divinity, one cannot but conclude that the last words of the Vedas are those passages where each such deity is considered as only one expression of the same many-faceted supreme Almighty. One such passage from the Aitareya Upanishad raises the question: Who is this Self, whom we desire to worship? Is he the self by which we see, hear, etc.? Is he the heart and mind by which we perceive? No, says the Upanishad. These are but adjuncts of the Self. The Self itself is Pure Consciousness. He is *brahman*. He is God, He is Brahma, He is Indra, He is all Gods; the five elements – earth air space, water fire; all beings, great or small, born of eggs, born from the womb, born from heat, born from soil; horses, cows, men, elephants, birds; everything that breathes, the beings that walk and the beings that walk not, the beings that fly and those that fly not. The reality behind all these is *brahman*, who is pure Consciousness. Consciousness is *brahman*.

The natural state of each individual is the state of being *brahman*, say the scriptures. Sankara therefore defines *bhakti* in specific terms as contemplative living in one's natural state, that is, the divine state. This *brahma-bhAva*, being in *brahman*, automatically implies an equanimous view of every being in the world as the same self as the one dwells in the seer. This balanced view of everything as One, everything as the Self, is a blissful experience, called *brahma-Ananda*. It does not come out of studies or scholarship. It is a state to be enjoyed internally, not by the external apparatus. When that experience crystallises, there is no more knowledge, no more ignorance, no perceiver, nothing perceived, no perception. All that is seen by these enlightened souls is the godliness of Infinite Love and the loveliness of the Omnipresent God.

Sankara waxes eloquent about such a state of supreme *bhakti, which we call advaita bhakti,* in glowing terms. This poetic but precise description of Sankara is very often quoted as the thesis on *bhakti*. It is verse no.61 of *SivAnanda-lahari*. It gives five analogies for *bhakti* or Devotion to Divinity. The first one cites what is called an ankola tree which has the characteristic that when its seeds fall from the tree on the ground and mature, they travel to the base of the tree and join the roots by their own nature. Just as these seeds reach the tree with a one-pointed purpose, so also the devotee should be devoted to his God of devotion – is the theme. The second analogy is that of iron filings that are drawn to a magnet. In these two analogies the duality of the components of the system involved is all but obvious. The next two analogies are that of a chaste wife being devoted and drawn towards her husband and that of a creeper which winds around a parent tree. In these two cases the quality of the relationship is certainly different from that of the first two analogies but still some duality remains. The fifth analogy is that of a river which is irrevocably bound to a path towards the ocean, its ultimate destination. It appears it is this analogy that is closest to the heart of Adi Sankara as far as his definition of *bhakti* is concerned.

Think of a golden ring. Does gold have the form of a ring? Goldness has nothing to do with the shape of a ring or roundness. The roundness of the ring is extraneous to gold. Do not see the ring, see only the gold, they say. This is why even words fail when the Vedas want to describe the Ultimate. What is not spoken by the tongue but what makes the tongue speak is *brahman*, not the thing that is before you, says K.U.. It is something which the words cannot describe, eyes cannot see, the ears cannot hear. Even the senses cannot sense it. How can the Seer see himself? How can the Knower know himself? So somehow out of all the multiplicity that is visible to us we have to see and sense the unity which is our own Self.

Jiva and Jivatma

The Superior Shakti (parA-prakRRiti = parA-shakti = chit-shakti)) inherent in Brahman contributes to the spark of the spiritual undercurrent vibrating in each living being (B.G. VII – 5). This spark is only a tiny fragment (B.G. X – 42). It is called the Jiva, the individual soul. It is Matter, in association with Spiritual Energy. This Spiritual 'Energy' (I am using the word 'Energy' for want of a better word. Don't bring in your scientific notions here!) is the JivAtmA. Actually it should simply be called 'AtmA', but when our discussion centres round an individual we call it 'JivAtmA'.

So, to summarise, Jiva is Matter in association with Spiritual Energy. Also, Spiritual Energy under a material envelope. Note that JIva is under the constant spell of mAyA or avidyA.

Ishvara is Spiritual Energy viewed in relation to Matter. In other words it is Brahman conditioned by our intellect. Note that it is in complete control of mAyA or avidyA.

Jiva is not the Self (=Atman). It is the empirical self. Or the individual soul. Jiva, usually knows things the wrong way. For example it identifies itself with the body, mind, intellect (BMI). And another mistake, it uses the word 'I' for itself invariably. Thus jIva makes the mistake of identifying 'I' (Ramana Maharshi's 'I') with the BMI in which it resides. That Jiva is knowing everything the wrong way dawns on it only when true enlightenment illumines it. How long has it been knowing things in the wrong away? Ever since it became the Jiva. When did it become the Jiva? When Ignorance descended on it. Whose Ignorance? Jiva's ignorance. Thus Ignorance and Jiva are coeval. You cannot say which was first. Vedanta says this is undecidable (*anirvacaniyam*) But when finally enlightenment comes to the Jiva, there is no more Jiva thereafter. Only Brahman/ Atman.

The JIva (the soul) is the subject of all experience. It is a complex of Consciousness (*ChaitanyaM*) and Matter. When objects are in relation to the subject we have the stream of presentations called

Vrittis. When there are no objects there will be no presentations but the consciousness that lights up the presentations will remain. That consciousness is the Witness, the non-participating Witness. Objects are not presented to Consciousness as such. They are directly presented to the JIva (the soul) and only indirectly to the Witness. There can be no relationship between Consciousness and objects, because they belong to different orders of reality, like the rope and the snake. The subject, the centre of consciousness, is experienced directly in an intuition, like an 'I-feeling' *(aham-pratyaya),* but the object is known only from the outside like 'this-feeling' *(idam-pratyaya)*.

Then how did this Pure Consciousness become the JIva or the empirical self and how was the JIva made the subject of all experience? Strictly speaking, there is no 'becoming, no making, no transition, no transformation'. Pure Consciousness (Atman, Brahman) does not undergo any change of form or character. JIva is only Brahman in an empirical dress of BMI in which the sprouting of the thought of distinctness from Brahman has occurred. This thought of individuality is the Ego, the starting point of the JIva. JIva is therefore Consciousness conditioned by Ignorance in the form of an ego of individuality. The Self can have no direct knowledge of the world except through the apparatus of the BMI. This apparatus as well as the small world which becomes the object of its knowledge is spoken of as the adjunct (*upAdhi)* of Consciousness. All this adjunct is matter. Consciousness ('*Chaitanyam*') which has this limited portion of matter for its adjunct is the JIva. Each JIva has its own knowing apparatus and moves in a small world of its own, with its own joys and sorrows and thus has its own individual existence. Though the Self is one, the JIvas are many.

Shankara draws attention to this fact of one Self and several JIvas, for instance, in his commentary on (B.G.2-12) where the Lord saysThere was never a time when I was not there nor you were not there, nor these leaders of men nor that we, all of us, will come to be hereafter. He comments 'The plural number (in we) is used following the diversity of the bodies, but not in the sense of the multiplicity of the Self'. (d*eha-bhedAnuvRttyA bahu-vacanaM, na Atma-bhedAbhipreyA*) Generally in his commentaries, Shankara uses two illustrations to bring home this point. One is the sun appearing as many reflected images in different pools of water. If the waters are dried up the several images get back to the original sun. The other illustration is the infinite space being delimited by artificial barriers. If these barriers are knocked down there will be no occasion to speak of the different spaces. These two illustrations of the exact mode of conceiving the relation between the Self (AtmA, or also the JivAtmA, if the context permits it) and the Soul (Jiva) gave rise to two schools of argument in later advaita, namely, the argument of original and its reflection (*bimba-pratibimba-vAda*), and the the argument of delimitation (*avaccheda-vAda*). The former is the VivaraNa school and the latter is the BhAmati school.

Thus when Consciousness is conditioned by its association with Ignorance or Matter it is no longer Pure Consciousness but a complex of both, called JIva, the soul. This does not mean however that Matter or Ignorance is outside of the Reality of Consciousness, because that would contradict non-duality. The relation between Self (Atman) and Soul (Jiva) has therefore to be conceived in the following way.

The addition of the adjunct is only a difference in the standpoint that we adopt. There are two standpoints – the intuitive and the intellectual. The intuitive is that of immediate and direct realisation. It is the method of the mystics. There is no dualism of subject and object there, nor that of doer and the deed, nor that of agent and enjoyer. These distinctions of duality arise only in the intellectual method of looking at reality. That is why the Gita says that it is "beyond the intellect" (III – 43). It is the nature of the intellect to break up the original unity and revel in these distinctions. At this intellectual level what we are doing is actually a come-down in the level of perception. The JIva is now perceived in relation to its own small world, the subject in relation to the object and the doer in relation to the deed. The Self thus reflected in the medium of the intellect becomes the JIva. As per the VivaraNa school, the Atman or the Self is the original, the intellect is the reflecting medium and the JIva is the reflected image. In the case of the BhAmati school, the Atman is the infinite space, the adjuncts (*upAdhis*) are the limiting barriers and the JIvas are the small spaces.

The JIva is thus a complex of Consciousness (*Chaitanyam)* and matter. It is Pure Consciousness with a limited adjunct of matter, namely, the BMI. This limited adjunct is spoken of as the Ignorance (*avidyA*) of the JIva. Stripped of its adjunct the JIva loses its individuality and is then nothing but Pure ChaitanyaM. The analysis of the three states of waking, dreaming and sleeping is intended to show that Consciousness is the only constant factor running through them all. It is in the fourth state called 'turIya', that transcends the three states of waking, dream and dreamless sleep, all traces of Ignorance disappear. When the JIva is thus disassociated from Ignorance and therefore from all material vesture, the spiritual core of the JIva comes into its own. Shankara sets forth (in his commentary on Br.Su. I-3-19) the nature of this transcendence of all adjuncts in the following way. A white crystal placed by the side of something red or blue appears red or blue on account of the adjunct. But in reality the crystal is only white. It does not 'acquire' its white colour but only shines in its own natural colour.

Before the onset of true enlightenment the Spirit (Consciousness) on account of its association with the BMI appears as the JIva. But the rise of true knowledge does make a real difference.

All false notions disappear and Spirit rises to its true stature. The self-hood of the empirical self falls to the ground and the Self shines forth in its original splendour. To know the highest truth is only to know the self in its true nature. The moment true enlightenment dawns on man he realises that he is no other than the non-dual self, that very moment he sheds his finitude and rises to his full stature. There is no question of the JIva merging in anything other than itself. It simply comes to its own.

In truth there is no entity as the JIva at all. It is not among the things created. It is a false creation due entirely to adventitious ('Agantuka') or incidental circumstance, that is, coming from without and not pertaining to the fundamental nature. "The idea of embodiedness is a result of nescience. Unless it be through the false ignorance of identifying the Self with the body, there can be no embodiedness for the Self" *('sa-sharIratvasya mithyA-jnAna-niimittatvAt .... kalpayituM':* Shankara's Commentary on Br. Su. I-1-4). JIva has always remained Brahman. Only the adjuncts have to be removed for this truth to stand out. Once this realisation is there, the finitude of the JIva will disappear, as also its misery and its supposed agency and enjoyership. "When that Brahman, the basis of all causes and effects, becomes known, all the results of the seeker's actions become exhausted" (Mu.U. II–2-8). The transmigration of the JIva which is due to its false association with the adjuncts, will also come to a close. That is when the ego-thought of separateness from the Supreme Self, with an 'I' of its own, will get destroyed. That is what we mean by saying 'JIva attains mokSha'. The two things are simultaneous, like the simultaneity of disappearance of darkness with the lighting of a match. But that does not mean that JIva 'reaches some destination' or 'obtains something'. 'JIva sees the Truth' simply means that it sees that it is itself Brahman. In other words, it wakes up to the Truth that was always there. Not waking up to the Truth was the Ignorance. Ignorance is not in Brahman, which is pure and self-illumined, but in the JIva. So long however as the latter does not realize his identity with Brahman, ignorance is said, rather loosely, to envelop Brahman.

All the injunctions that are given by the Vedas to man are given to him in his state of ignorance because activity is natural to man in that state. The Self is never the doer. The injunction is only a restatement following what is given in experience. All the ritual purifications through chanting of mantras and the results of such actions are enjoined on, and enjoyed by, that entity which has the idea "I am the doer", as stated in the Mundaka Upanishad (M.U.) mantra "One of the two enjoys the fruits having various tastes, while the other looks on without enjoying" (Mu. U. III-1-1). The misery that falls to the lot of the JIva, the empirical self, is entirely due to its fancied association with its adjuncts. This association imagines such 'realities' as 'I am a brahmin', 'I am a renunciate', 'I am a JIva' and the like. When the JIva sheds these imagined realities and all adventitious adjuncts(=*upAdhis*) and realises its true nature by a discrimination between the permanent and the ephemeral, then there is an end of all its misery. Except by such knowledge of the Ultimate Self, misery and finitude cannot be overcome.

Postscript: Just a note on '*ahaM brahma asmi'*. 'ahaM' is the Self without the upAdhis (=adjuncts) in association with the individual – in fact, without anything that can attribute to oneself. So 'ahaM' is the JivAtman'. 'brahma' is the Supreme Absolute without the upAdhis of mAyA. These two are one and the same. This is the *Jiva-brahma aikyam* that advaita propagates as the teaching of the Upanishads. It is also referred to in the scriptures as *'JivAtma-paramAtma-aikyaM'*.

Saguna Brahman and Nirguna Brahman

Ishvara, otherwise well-known as God Supreme, is another way of referring to Saguna brahman. The deities in our temples, the *vigrahas* that we worship at home, and the God to whom we appeal in distress, saying 'Oh God, Save Me!' … These are all Saguna brahman. They have a name – in fact several several names — a form and packages of attributes – which together give lots of ideas for artists to make excellent paintings and pictures. The entire world of Hindu scriptures is brimming with anecdotes and episodes of al these deities and gods. Each one of these gods and deities also corresponds to the God Supreme of the other religions.

Now come to Nirguna brahman, otherwise also referred to as the Supreme Absolute. ParamAtmA is the only other name with which sometimes it is referred to. Otherwise it has no multiplicity of names. Definitely no form. And no attributes of any kind. If you still want to associate some kind of an 'attribute' to it it is only to say 'it has no second'. It is only one of its kind.

There is a wrong understanding that we humans and other beings are all certain parts of Brahman. If you are talking of Nirgunabrahman, this is wrong, because brahman has no parts.. The Absolute Nirgunabrahman is a concept which is not easily understood by beginners in Advaita. The human beings that we are, when we refer to ourselves as I we are not referring to the Brahman which is our real Self. We are referring only to the conglomeration of the body, mind, intellect that we are. This is what is called our outer self. There is an inner Self which has nothing to do with anything that we call ours. This is the most difficult point to understand in Vedanta. We certainly are brahman ("*ahaM brahma asmi*") but in order to understand this sentence "I am brahma', we have to throw away all that goes with 'I' in our usual parlance. Then what remains is Brahman, the Self! So the 'Self; has nothing to do with our name, our address our position, our character, our

Having understood that there are two kinds of brahman, as explained in the 1st article, now let us see where stands the universe of objects. We see millions of objects in the universe, including our own human beings and other living beings. Just as we human beings, each of us wihout exception, have an immanent presence of the absolute brahman in us, the universe of objects also has this immanent presence. Immanence is the word. This word has generally no importance for other religions, because they do not think of their god without form or attributes. Even the deities in our temples have the immanent presence of the absolute brahman. Whatever you see is Brahman in its immanent presence in the object you see. The object you see, including the universe, is only mAyA. This mAyA is the shakti of Brahman and it is what expresses itself as everything in the world, including the objects you, including the saguna brahman you worship. The effect of mAya is, what you see is not absolutely real, it is only an experience and nothing more — like the movie we see on a screen.

Now let us understand two important words often occurring in Vedanta. One is the word 'transcendental' and the other is the word 'transactional'. The absolute Brahman (Nirguna brahman) is the transcendental truth whereas the universe within which we operate is only a transactional (operational) truth. The transactional truth ultimately turns out to be no truth at all, because it disappears. The transactional truth is like the roles that the same actor appears in different TV serials. In one serial he may be the husband of an actress and in another serial he may be the brother of the same actress playing a different role. Any one who confuses the transactional and the transcendental truths will have to go a long way. He is the one who comes out with the question: If you say there is only one absolute God, then why do you go and worship different Gods in temples? Mixing up of the transactional and transcendental truth is the problem. These are the people who ask you: Which is greater? Saguna brahman or Nirguna brahman? Saguna brahman is the voluntary show-off of mAyA. Even within it there is the immanent presence of Nirguna-brahman. Each transactional object in the world, whether it is a material object or whether it is a divine deity should be understood to have the transcendental truth immanent in it, inspite of the outer visibility. This is the beauty of the concept of immanence.

यच्च किम्चिज्जगत् सर्वम् दृश्यते श्रूयतेपि वा अन्तर्बहिश्च तत्सर्वं व्याप्य नारायण स्थितः

yacca kimcijjagat sarvam dRRishyate shrUte. pi va / antar-bahishca tatsarvaM vyApya nArAyana sthitah –

says the M.N.U. So in every object we should be able to see the godly presence. That is why when we say namaste to others, we must remember it is actually addressed to the immanent absolute embedded in the other person just as the immanent presence of the Self in us.

The conflict about the antithesis between the impersonal and personal facets of God would vanish if one studies *Narayaneeyam.* carefully and understands how Bhattatiri can extol both the facets to the skies equally strongly.

The Ultimate Reality is non-dual. Reality is only one – in the sense there is Reality and Reality alone. To name it by something is an under-statement. To give it a form again circumscribes it. It is actually nameless and formless. It just exists. **It is Consciousness; it is Bliss**, say the scriptures. This non-duality that is the central core of *advaita* philosophy therefore identifies the Supreme Self (that transcends everything) with the innermost Self (that is immanent in every being). If God or the Supreme Reality does not have a separate status other than our Selves, then who is to worship whom? Hence the concept of Bhakti, or Devotion, seems to contradict the Oneness inherent in *advaita*. This apparent conflict may be easily resolved by studying *Narayaneeyam*.

That the Ultimate is non-dual there is no question. But to be able to realise it as a fact of experience one has to go through the processes of Bhakti of God with form and content, with name and description, with qualities and adjuncts. Such a God is *saguNa Brahman*, in contrast to the *nirguNa Brahman* which is the formless and nameless Absolute. Bhattattiri's conception of Bhakti emphasizes the *nirguNa* aspect of the Ultimate in no uncertain terms, even while he expatiates on the worship of the visible form. His rationale is summed up in verse no.10 of the 99th Dasaka.

The very idea of a second entity in existence introduces fear and insecurity. *But in practical life one has to accept duality and multiplicity.*

The concept of non-duality has to be only in one's attitude. The practical application of it is possible only for the few *JIvanmuktas* (= the liberated while still living) about whom history has select examples like **Sadasiva Brahmendra, Ramana MahaRshi** and **Ramakrishna Paramahamsa Kanchi mahA-swamigal. And Chandrasekhara Bharati Swamigal of Sringeri** Ordinary seekers can only pray to God to be given that equanimous view of everything that we see, hear or touch.). Be it friend or foe, be it human or animal, can we see all alike? This *samadRshTi* is attainable only by Service – Service to God and Man. So long as this equanimous view does not arise in the mind one has to keep striving and worshipping through the normal modes of devotion to forms and idols. These four *shloka*s constitute the essence of the teaching of *Narayaneeyam* for the layman. The basis of the teaching is *advaita* pure and simple. The means recommended is Bhakti.

This is a a SAGUNA-NIRGUNA SYNCRETIC PRAYER from Shankara.

मयूराधिरूढं महावाक्यगूढं मनोहारिदेहं महच्चित्तगेहम्।
महीदेवदेवं महावेदभावं महादेवबालं भजे लोकपालम् ॥

The explicit meaning of the verse is: I sing the praise of that protector of the world,

(*mayuradhiroodam*): Who has the peacock as his chariot,

(*mahavakyagoodam*): Who is the hidden import of the great Vedic declarations

(*manoharideham*): Who displays a wonderfully enchanting body

(*mahaccittageham*): Who dwells in the minds of great noble ones

(*mahidevadevam*): Who is the one supreme divinity of all the divines,

(*mahavedabhavam*): Who is the quintessence of the massive Vedas,

And who is the great son of Lord Shiva.

This is verse No.3 of Subrahmanya-bhujangam, a poem of praise composed and sung extempore by Adi Sankara before the Subrahmanya deity of Tiruchendur at the southern tip of India, where it meets the Indian Ocean. The poem itself has 33 verses. According to some traditions it is said that when Sri Sankara sang this particular verse Lord Subrahmanya gave him His divine darshan.

The three epithets *mayuradhiroodam, manoharideham,* and *mahidevadevam* profess the SAGUNA form of the Lord, by singing His external attributes.

The three epithets *mahavakyagoodam*, *mahaccittageham*, and *mahavedabhavam* profess the NIRGUNA character of the Lord Absolute.

The two types of epithets are symbiotically strung into the verse, one of each type in each quarter so that the lilting bhujanga-prayata (snake-movement-like) metre, which is the metre adopted in the whole poem, comes out with a majesty of its own.

The epithets mahadeva balam and lokapalam occurring in the last quarter do not belong to either type because they are definitely not talking about the formless Absolute nor do they indicate a form.

In this verse Sankara takes us as it were from the exterior to the interior, from the outer to the inner, from the gross to the subtle and from attributes to the Real Absolute. In fact the whole poem reveals the splendour, glory and Infinity of Lord Subrahmanya, both externally and internally. The very start of this verse has the word *mayuradhiroodam*, by which the symbol AUM of the vedas is indicated because of the very profile of the peacock. The peacock has a very small head, bent neck, spread feathers, one foot on the earth and the other foot slightly raised – put all these together you get the profile of the pranava mantra of Vedanta.

Let me convey my indebtedness to Ramanathan Palaniappan's book in Tamil entitled *Tiruchendurin kadalorathil* for the above ideas on this shloka.

One of the beauties of Hinduism is that it teaches us that, while God is infinitely higher than ourselves, He is also infinitely near to us. He is nearer to us than our hands and feet. He is the Soul of our souls. This concept of immanence is the strongest point of Sanatana Dharma. He is the one that survives in us from childhood to adulthood and through old age, from birth, as the I that we talk of when we refer to ourselves (7th shloka of Dakshinamurthi ashtakam of Shankara). He is neither the body nor the senses, nor the mind nor the ego, nor the intellect; He is the I that is none of these, but is far distant from anything that we can call ours in a related manner like spouse, issue, wealth, possessions and so forth (1st shloka of *Advaita-pancharatnam* of Shankara). He is the ever-present witness to all our experiences. He is really our Atman. He is Brahman. He is the One Reality beyond which there is none. Brahman and Atman differ, if at all, only in our approach. Atman is the name given to the highest Reality if we seek one such within ourselves. Brahman is the name given to the highest Reality if we seek one such in the universe. The greatest revelation of the Upanishads is the essential identity between Brahman (also denoted by the word *paramAtman*) and Atman (also known by the word *jIvAtman*, or the soul) as revealed by the grand mystic pronouncements called the *mahAvAkyas* of the four Vedas. Once the identity is established, the two terms become interchangeable and it makes no difference whether we speak of the Absolute of the Upanishads as Brahman or Atman.

But even though Godhead is so near to all of us, it is very difficult to realise Him. This is because we have to cease to be ourselves before we can know Him as He is. The difficulty in this concept is the fact that God is both transcendent and immanent. The immanence aspect is inbuilt into the concept of Atman and the transcendence aspect in the concept of Brahman. The scriptures, particularly the Upanishads and the Gita share with us their dilemma in having to describe both these aspects simultaneously. They adopt one of two alternatives. On the one hand they use the superlatives of all the qualities they can think of:

It is smaller than the smallest, bigger than the biggest, it is that which is supreme, than which there is nothing higher, than which there is nothing more minute, than which there is nothing more comprehensive (M.N.U).

He strides the entire universe, He is the purest of the pure, most auspicious of all that is auspicious, the God of Gods, the Imperishable Father of all Beings. (Preliminary shlokas to V.S).

On the other hand they use negation of all the finite things that we are capable of expressing:

whatever cannot be indicated by speech but that motivates all speech, that is Brahman; whatever cannot be seen by the eyes, but by which the eye sees, that is Brahman; not that which is worshipped (K.U);

neither internal consciousness nor external consciousness nor both; not a bundle of consciousness either; not the conscious One nor the non-conscious One; cannot be perceived, cannot be related, cannot be handled, cannot be attributed, cannot be indicated, nor can it be an object of thought (M.U.)

When the scriptures use negatives like these we should not take them to mean that Brahman is just a complete negation. It only means that our finite expressions can never do full justice to the infinite grandeur that is God, that God is wholly other than what we know in the world. He is the unifying principle behind all creatures. He is the canvas on which we shine as painted pictures.

Divine will and Free will. When the shastras say satyam vada, dharmam cara, there is an implication by the shastras that you and I have the free will to act otherwise also. Besides this free will, there is another power within us for which we are ourselves the architect, by means of the way we thought and acted in all our previous lives upto now. This is what is known as *prArabdha-karma*.,

Secondly, if there is only one absolute Brahman and everything else is only an appearance that comes and goes, where is the question of divine will? Does Brahman, the attributeless, have a will for itself? If it has, does it not contradict the oneness of Advaita? The divine will, if at all there is one, has to be only that of the saguNa-brahman. The question itself arises only when we make the standard mixing up of two levels of awareness. At the level of the Nirguna-brahman there is nothing else to talk about. But when we think of God or Ishvara, we have come down to the level of the transactional world and God is now nothing but saguNa brahman, with creations, with divine will, free will and so on.

Fate and Free will are interwoven just as the threads of a fabric are crossed and interlaced. We cannot rewrite our past or fly like a bird or breathe under water. These are our limitations, inherent in our nature, our fate. Our past is our fate for the future. But it is only our tendencies that are determined by our past (and the so-called fate). Our actions are not determined by our fate. Actions are ours.: Fate has nothing to do with it. Fate, that is, our *prArabdha*, might have created the circumstances that led to our action, but the action is ours. Fate might have contributed by shaping our tendencies, which led to our action, but the action is still ours. It is our mind that dictates our action. All spiritual teaching pleads for the Will of Man to become stronger than the mind. Everywhere in the upanishads the appeal is to the will. It is not as if man is a helpless creature as a leaf in the storm or a feather in the wind. Man's will has an element of complete freedom. It is the power which enables him to act in directions opposite even to his spontaneous bad tendency (*dur-vAsanA*). In this sense he is the architect of his fate. Indeed this is the time when he should not slacken any of his self-effort. Ultimately man's will must prove stronger than fate, because it is his own past will that created his present fate. Now the second line of shloka 33 of B.G. Ch.11, namely mayaivete nihatAH pUrvameva reiterates the power of divine will over personal will.

Ravana was *ahamkAra* personified, and even for Rama it was no easy task. For this direct confrontation with *ahaMkAra* we need to be aware of our own real nature, *sat-cit-Ananda,* that is, *Brahman*. *Brahman*'s power can be spoken of in two ways. One is known as *parAshakti*; Its innate nature is j*nAna*. It is also known as *VidyA* (knowledge) and also as *cit-shakti* (Absolute

Consciousness). The manifestation of this is the duo of *JIva* and *Ishvara*. Gita calls it *Purushha* or *kshetrajna*. The other Power of *Brahman* is known as *aparA-shakti*. Its nature is inert. It has several other names such as, *PrakRRiti* (Cosmic Nature), *avyaktaM* (the unmanifest), *avidyA* (Ignorance) and MAyA (an untranslatable word). This is what gives rise to the five fundamental elements and therefrom the entire universe.

When this *avyaktaM* in its equilibrium stage where all the three guNas are equally poised (*guNa-sAmyaM*) is one with *cit-shakti,* then there is no *vikAra* of anything ; that *citshakti i*s known as the *para-rUpa* of *Brahman*. In other words, it is the *nirguNa Brahman*, to be realised and known. When the Absolute Consciousness is associated with the *Sattva*-dominated *avyaktaM,* that is called the *apara-rUp*a of *Brahman*; also known as *saguNa-brahma*n. This is the *Ishvara* with all infinite qualities (and also the God of all other religons) and is to be worshipped and meditated on. This is what shines in our *hRRiidayAkAsha* with the light of a thousand suns, so to say

This is the Aditya that we propitiate every day. The Vedas mention this Aditya as residing in our *hRRidayAkAsha. asau Adityo brahmaivAhamasmi* (Part of Sandhyavandana-mantras). And Agastya uses his Adityahridayam to remind Rama of His divinity.

Vision of Equanimity is Practical Non-Duality

How does an *advaitin* (=he who follows the *advaita* or non-dual school) live? Practical non-duality is what he would practise or want to practise. He is convinced that there exists nothing but the Absolute Self. It is the immutable infinite beyond anything described by words or delimited by attributes. It is also the immanent entity in anything that is perceivable by the senses. But this theoretical conviction seems to have only a nebulous contact with the diverse goings-on of this outward self with which we exist, converse, act and experience. One is not sure what it means for this conviction to percolate into one's activities. The seeker, who has just been exposed to the fundamentals of *advaita* has a tendency to feel that it is only a thought-concept and may not be applicable to this 'world of multiplicity'. His logic is that if one considers everybody else and everything else to be nothing but his own self then the ordinary relationships in the material world would all collapse. Some random thoughts on these matters have been gathered by me over the years from famous exponents of advaita who were also, in some sense, practitioners of what they preached. The most important of them, at least for me, happened to be my father (Sri R.Visvanatha Sastri: 1882 – 1956), from whom I learnt most of what I think I know today. The example being my father, I could take lessons from the way he himself reacted to multifarious daily situations in public and private life.

There are two things: *kriyAdvaita* – advaita in action – and *bhavAdvaita* – advaita in attitude. As in almost all spheres and facets of the *sanAtana dharma*, it is the attitude that is more important. Even in the secular world the criminal law dispenses a softer punishment to someone who kills, only accidentally and not with intent, than to the one who kills with intent. It is the attitude that matters. A convinced advitin has to have his right attitude reflect in all his day-to-day actions. It is the attitude of *sama-dRshTi*, that is, equanimous vision. The Gita couplet: He who sees Me everywhere, and who sees everything in Me, to him I am never lost nor is he lost to me:

यो मां पश्यति सर्वत्र सर्वम् च मयि पश्यति
तस्याहं न प्रणश्यामि स च मे न प्रणश्यति

yo mAm pashyati sarvatra sarvam ca mayi pashyati /
tasyAham na praNashyAmi sa ca me na praNashyati //

This is not just a good quote for platform speeches. It is the ace-commandment from the Lord. It is practical advaita. Let us spend a few moments getting this straight.

This *advaita* attitude is just the awareness of the One Ultimate Reality which is both transcendent and immanent. Every time we pray to God or worship Him it should be with the conscious step of accepting a duality for the sake of worldly worship while in reality there is no duality. The sixteen formalities that are built into a *pUjA* are all expressions of this coming down, namely, a confession: Oh God! I cannot but worship You as someone separate from me but let this worship strengthen the realisation in me of the identity between You and my Inner Self. This is a characteristic of a true practitioner of advaita. It is clear that this is walking on razor's edge. When love of a *saguNa*-idol matures into Supreme Love of God, one sees the entire world as Himself. Love towards one object, and for the same reason, hate towards another object – this pattern will then give place to an infinite Love which sees no high and low, no distinction of duality. Love of God maturing into the insight of seeing the entire world as Himself is *advaita bhakti*.

This is where the first lesson of practical *advaita* starts. Normally when we think of another person, we tend to think of his negatives also. Very often only his negatives come to our mind rather than the good things about him. But the habit of seeing God in everybody should be practised in such a way that the first thing that we attempt to do is to forget the negatives of the other person. When we think of ourselves we very often forget our own negatives. Even when another person points it out to us we tend to either ignore it or disbelieve it. The advaitic injunction of seeing ourselves in the other person, when translated into action, gives us the lever to ignore or forget his negatives just as we do with our own thus setting up almost a supernatural empathy with the other person.. If this happens to the majority of us, half the world's problems are solved. This is the first great leap forward in spirituality.

The next step is to see the same God in all Gods and Divinities. The dogmatism that is inherent in the fanatical love of one's own religion or in such love of one's own school of philosophy should give way to look at all paths to God as valid and of value.

The third and final step is what is described in the 6th and 7th verses of the IshAvAsyopanishad:

यस्तु सर्वाणि भूतानि आत्मन्येवानुपश्यति
सर्व-भूतेषु चात्मानं ततो न विजुगुप्सते
यस्मिन् सर्वाणि भूतानि आत्मैवाभूद्विजानतः
तत्र को मोहः कः शोकः एकत्वं अनुपश्यतः

'yastu sarvANi bhUtAni Atmany-evAnupashyati;
sarva-bhUteshu cAtmAnaM tato na vijugupsate //
yasmin sarvANi bhUtAni AtmaivAbhUd-vijAnataH;
tatra ko mohaH kaH shokaH ekatvaM anupashyataH //'

Meaning: He who sees all beings in the Self and the Self in all beings, hates none; to the illumined soul, who sees everything as a manifestation of his own Self, how can there be delusion or grief since he sees only oneness? Even here the seers have advised us to proceed in two stages. The first stage for this conceptual identification of vision is a sense of unity with other existences. This unity makes us give respect to everything. The next stage is to identify it with the Self. The respect shown to other beings now widens into compassion and love to the things in which we see our own Self. But this oneness is still only an artificial oneness, a pluralistic unity. Real knowledge begins with a perception, not just an understanding at the intellectual level, of this oneness. The concept of pluralistic unity must give place, or lead to, a total comprehension or perception in the experiential level. To do this one has to first retreat from the outside world – *nivRtti*. Then see everything in Oneself. The opposite of this is a narrow I-feeling; that is what causes attachment and hate. The spiritual disciplines purify one's mind and this coupled with the association of the *sAtvic* type of people lead to an illumination which unfolds the harmony of one-ness. This is the vision. After this vision, the world from which one has retreated is drawn into the Self. Ethically the formula is: Detach yourself attitudinally, and then Love. Live in that dynamic unity. No more separate self, no more likes and dislikes, no more hopes and fears. This is the only way of serving society, says Swami Vivekananda. This equanimity of vision is the rationale for the commandment of Jesus: Love thy neighbour. When such an illumination of Oneness and Equanimity arrives where is the possibility of grief or delusion? Grief is always about an event in the past. Delusion is in the present. Fear is about the future. It is the Lord who is the Master of the past, present and future. – *bhUta-bhavya-bhavat-prabhuH.* For one who has given himself up to the Lord of the past, present and future, there is no grief, no delusion, no fear. Such a one is a *vijAnat*, the one who knows, who sees with a distinguished vision, whose conviction is not just at an academic level, but is of personal experience born out of inner conviction. For such a one there is only the Self – no non-Self.

But all this is a tall order. Every one agrees, including the stalwarts of *advaita* themselves. They all agree that the prerequisite to this vision is a life of devotion not only to the Personal Ultimate but also to the duties enjoined by one's calling and nature. And further they all agree that for those fortunate and blessed ones for whom the vision of Oneness has been gained, the life of devotion will be natural to them though not a life of enjoined action.

It is interesting to recall a few great stalwarts here. Listen to Madhusudana Saraswati, the confirmed advaitin who says that recalling the vision of the blue-eyed Krishna and his pranks is more interesting and fascinating rather than living in the vision of the unparallelled Glory and Light of the Ultimate.:

Seated in meditation, their minds totally absorbed in that Supreme Unmanifested Reality, which is changeles, attributeless and actionless, let the Yogis see that mystic Glory of Light which they seem to visualise; but, for us mortals, we should only yearn that there may miraculously appear before our physical eyes that bluish someone who keeps romping on the shores of the Yamuna:

ध्यानावस्थित-तद्गतेन मनसा तम् निर्गुणम् निष्क्रियम्
ज्योतिः किम्चन योगिनो यदि पुनः पश्यन्ति पश्यन्तु ते
अस्माकं तु तदेव लोचन चमत्कराय भूयात् चिरं
कालिन्दी पुलिनेषु यत्किमपि तम् नीलम् तमो धावति

dhyAnAvasthita-tadgatena manasA tam
nirguNam nishkriyam
jyotiH kimcana yogino yadi punaH
pashyanti pashyantu te /
asmAkam tu tadeva locana camatkarAya
bhUyAt ciram
kALindI pulineshu yatkimapi tam nIlam
tamo dhAvati //

Listen to Bhatttadri, the famous Kerala scholar of the 17th century, in his masterly epitome of Srimad-*Bhagavatam*. What is Fear? Fear occurs when we are conscious of another object different from oneself. This consciousness of duality is itself an imagination of the mind. I am trying my best through my discrimination to discipline the mind in the consciousness of Oneness. But when my mind is overpowered by your *mAyA*, the effort is of no avail. Therefore, Oh Lord, I am trying to overcome the fear (caused by duality) by constant and devoted worship of Thyself.

It is clear therefore that the vision of Oneness is not supposed to be obtained by just the snap of a finger – unless the Lord wills it, of course. The utmost that one can do is to seek the Grace of the Lord by a total surrender *without any expectation of what may or may not happen*. It is this surrender that is so nicely dramatised in the episode of *dAmodara* in the Krishnavatara: As a child Krishna was so mischievous that His mother had no alternative but to tie Him up. She used several ropes but failed. When she was totally exasperated she just gave up as if in surrender to the child. And then it was that the Lord decided to get himself bound and He allowed Himself to be tethered. Incidentally this gave him the name: *dAmodara*, the one who submitted to the rope round his waist. The esoteric lesson of this episode is that we should surrender to the Lord totally.

Vedanta Sopanam in 27 Shlokas

(वेदान्त-सोपानं)

A Vedanta staircase spiritually graded for appropriate ages

This is an unusual compilation of 27 Sanskrit shlokas with vedantic content starting from the rock-bottom base to a spiritual height. The grading of the shlokas is for five age-levels, namely, 5, 20, 40, 60 and 80. One has to first assimilate the meanings and contents of the shlokas pertaining to lower age levels than one's own.. And then it is time for him to rise to the next age level. Each shloka (except the first, which is only a list of God's names) is commented upon with a detailed English meaning. The whole thing is an epitome of Vedanta in its entirety without any dilution. If one starts from the beginning, assimilating the matter allotted to lower age levels, by the time one reaches the final level one would have the knowledge of an enlightened jnAni. Whether he has actually become one will however be dependent on his own self-effort and Grace of God.

The shlokas are from

1. **Achyutashtakam**
2. **Bhartrhari's Vairagyashatakam**
3. **Shivanandalahari**
4. **Prahladastuti in Bhagavatam**
5. **Hitopadesa**
6. **Bhoja charita**
7. **Valmiki Ramayana**

---

8. **Chandogya Upanishad**
9. **Kapila Gita in Bhagavatham**
10. **Shivamanasa puja of Shankara**
11. **Vivekachudamani**
12. **Shatashloki of Shankara**
13. **Narayaneeyam**
14. **Kathopanishad**

---

15. **Shivanandalahari**
16. **Aghamarshana suktam of Yajur veda**
17. **Dhruvastuti of Bhagavatam**

18. **Nasadiyasuktam of Rigveda**
19. **Panchadashi**
20. **Shruti gita of Bhagavatam**
21. **Vaidyanatha ashtakam**

---

22. **Advaita pancharatnam**
23. **Bhagavad Gita**
24. **Mukundamala of Kulasekhara**
25. **Gangashtakam of Shankara**
26. **Nirvanashatkam of Shankara**
27. **Hanuman chalisa**

Foreword to this single essay by Dr. K. Aravinda Rao,

(Retd. Director-General of Police, A.P. and Expositor at www.advaita.academy.org)

This essay with about 30 pages on Vedanta sopanam is a prescription for the use of a parent to guide all youngsters. This is a time-tested spiritual menu which was administered to all kids born in the generation of Prof. VK. Those like me, born about twenty years later, had a somewhat similar regimen.

There is abundant literature in our tradition which is meant to teach people of all ages. There are texts which can be enjoyed by the young and old alike. The stories of Gajendra or Prahlada, or taming of Kaliya in Srimad Bhagavatam can be enjoyed by a five year old; they can be enjoyed by an adult and they are read with devotion by a philosopher. The same verses give deeper and deeper meanings as a mature mind churns them.

The teacher in Prof. VK is highly passionate and concerned about the emotional and spiritual training of young minds. He finds newer and newer ways of presenting his syllabus. In this book he has identified five periods in life and prescribed the menu. A guru is like a gardener who closely watches the ripening of a fruit from time to time and takes care to nourish or put pesticides to kill any problem. In this book we have verses from a wide variety of texts - Hitopadesam, Vairagya satakam, Bhoja Prabandha, Bhagavatam, Veda, Shatashloki, Upanishad, Nasadiya suktam of Rigveda, all selected with a specific purpose, for nourishment, for overcoming obstacles.

As a person matures, the text may or may not remain the same, but the objective changes. We see that the final verses are for what Vedanta calls nididhyasanam, contemplating the unity of self with Brahman. That is done by devotion to the Lord, the anchor who makes the seeker cross the ocean of existence.

K. Aravinda Rao

Twenty-seven SHLOKAS TO BE ASSIMILATED AT FIVE DIFFERENT AGE LEVELS OR EARLIER

Each age level should assimilate the shlokas for all the earlier levels! — so that one can remember the substance of all the twenty-seven shlokas at the onspot of the final journey!

Age five and above

1. Achyutashtakam

अच्युतं केशवं रामनारायणं कृष्ण दामोदरं वासुदेवं हरिं।
श्रीधरं माधवं गोपिकावल्लभं जानकी नायकं रामचन्द्रं भजे

achyutaM keshavaM rAmanArAyaNam kRRishhNa-dAmodaraM vAsudevaM hariM.
shrIdharaM mAdhavaM gopikAvallabhaM jAnakInAyakaM rAmachandraM bhaje

This has nothing but God's names in it. So there is no question of any meaning. The very names will do the magic of internal transformation!

Slokas 2 to 7 To be understood and assimilated before age 20:

By age 20 one gets an idea of the enormity of material things to be learnt and also has a taste of the inevitable power of the senses to detract us towards sensual pleasures. These six shlokas are deliberately pin-pointed to tackle this early hurdles in life as well as the familiar proclivity to the so-called pleasures of 'possession'.

2. From Bhartrhari

आदित्यस्य गतागतैः अहरहः संक्षीयते जीवितं
व्यापारैर्बहु-कार्य-भार-गुरुभिः कालोपि न ज्ञायते।
दृष्ट्वा जन्म-जरा-विपत्ति-मरणं त्रासश्च नोत्पद्यते
पीत्वा मोह-मयीं प्रमाद-मदिरां उन्मत्त-भूतं जगत्॥

Adityasya gatAgataiH aharahaH
samkshhIyate jIvitaM
vyApArairbahukAryabhAragurubhiH
kAlo.api na ~jnayate
dRRishhTvA janma jarAvipatti maraNaM
trAsashcha notpadyate
pItvA mohamayIm pramAdamadirAM
unmattabhUtaM jagat

The Sun rises and sets. Day passes into night and night into day. But what is really happening is they are taking away our lives. We are not even aware of the passage of time. Such is our deep involvement in the weight of our businesses. We do not seem to get a jolt of fear even after watching, almost daily, the inescapable sequence of birth, old age, adversity, misfortune, disaster, failure and final death. We are just overdrunk with the delusion of attachment which is our own making.

3. From Adishankara's Shivananda lahari

सदा मोहाटव्याम् चरति युवतीनां कुच-
नटत्य्-आशा-शाखासु अटति झटिति स्वैरम्-अभितः
कपालिन् भिक्षो मे हृदय-कपिम्-अत्यन्त-चपलं
दृढं भक्त्या बद्ध्वा शिव भवद्-अधीनं कुरु विभो ।।

sadA mohATvyAMcarati yuvatInAM kucha-girau
naTatyAshAshAkhAsu aTati jhaTiti svaramabhitaH
kapAlin ikshho me hRRidayakapimatyantachapalaM
dhRRiDhaM bhaktyA badhvA shiva bhavadadhInaM kuru vibho

Oh Lord Shiva, (The mind) constantly dwells on the sensualities of the woman's form, (Look how Adi Shankara is taking our faults on himself!) and dances on the hopes and desires generated by such thoughts. Oh Lord with the skull as the begging bowl, please deign to bind my extremely fickle monkey-mind, tightly with (the rope of) devotion** and make it totally subservient to You!

4. Srimad Bhagavatham (VII-9-45) Prahladastuti

यन्-मैथुनादि गृह-मेधि सुखं हि तुच्छं
कण्डूयनेन करयोरिव दुःख-दुःखं।
तृप्यन्ति नेह कृपणा बहु-दुःख-भाजः
कण्डूतिवन् मनसिजं विषहेत धीरः॥

Yan-maithunAdi gRRihamedhi sukhaM hi tucchaM
kaNDUyanena karayoriva duHkha-duHkhaM.
tRRipyanti neha kRRipaNA bahu-duHkha-bhAjaH
kaNDUtivan manasijaM vishhaheta dhIraH.

** Note this word 'bhakti'. One would have expected Shankara to say 'jnana' here! But he knows '*bhaktyA mAm abhijAnati;*' (B,G. 18 – 55)

The pleasure that a householder obtains from sex is a trivial one; like scratching for the itching in the hands, it is only a chain of distress. Even after suffering repeated unhappiness, foolish ones do not cry a halt to the scratching-like pleasure. Only the brave soul overcomes what (lust) arises in the mind.

5. From Hitopadesha

आहार-निद्रा-भय-मैथुनं च सामान्यमेतत् पशुभिर्नराणाम्।
धर्मो हि तेषां अधिको विशेषः धर्मेण हीनाः पशुभिः समानाः॥

AhAranidrA bhayamaithunaM ca
sAmAnyametat pashubhirnarANAM.
Dharmo hi teshhAM adhiko visheshhaH
dharmeNa hInAH pashubhiH samAnAH.

Food, sleep, fear and reproduction are common to both animals and humans. What is extra for humans is dharma; without dharma man is nothing but an animal. Here Dharma is an amalgam of six virtues:

Self-confidence, fearlessness, *abhaya*;

Self-mastery, *dama;*

Self-integration, *Arjavam*, i.e., candour, straightforwardness, transparency;

Humility, modestry, *hrIH* (Feeling of a shame in doing wrong);

Purity, cleanlines of body, mind and speech ;

Compassion, dayA bhUteshu

6. From Bhoja carita

मान्धाता स महीपतिः कृतयुगालङ्कारभूतो गतः
सेतुर्येन महोदधौ विरचितः क्वासौ दशास्यान्तकः।
अन्ये चापि युधिष्टिर-प्रभृतयो याता दिवं भूपते
नैकेनापि समं गता वसुमती नूनं त्वया यास्यति॥

mAndhAtA sa mahIpatiH
kRRitayugAlankArabhUto gataH
seturyena mahodadhau viracitaH kvAsau
dashAsyAntakaH.
anye cApi yudhishTiraH prabRRitayo
yAtAdivam bhUpate
naikenApi samaM gatA vasumatI nUnaM
tvayA yAsyati

Absolute power corrupts absolutely. But a smart boy's four line shloka (given above) corrects it absolutely and becomes a permanent warning sign for all of us. The context is this. King Vatsa was the uncle of boy-Prince Bhoja. As the boy was a minor, his father on his death-bed made his brother Vatsa the guardian not only of the boy but of the kingdom, until the boy reached a proper age. But Vatsa planned a coup and forced his minister to take the boy to a forest, kill him, and bring the head to him as proof of the killing. The Minister had more sense. At the last moment in the forest, he tells the boy the truth. The boy writes the above shloka on a dry-leaf and gives it to the minister as a message to his uncle. The minister decides not to perform the bidding of the king, saves the boy, and brings a made-up head back to the King. The latter looks at what looks like the head of the boy, reads the message and immediately regrets his own action. The minister consoles him, manages a show of conjuring a sorceror's trick and brings back the real Bhoja, who later becomes the great King Bhoja-Raja of Ujjain.

Meaning of the shloka: The great King Mandhata, the gem of the Krita-yuga is gone;

The famous killer of the ten-faced Ravana, who was also the builder of the bridge across the ocean, is also no more; And others like Yudhishtira also have reached heaven; And none of these ever took this earth with them; but Oh king, certainly it is going to go with you!

This shloka should be able to detract your sense of craving for possession!

7. From Valmiki Ramayana:

नात्मनः कामकारोऽस्ति पुरुषोऽयमनीश्वरः। इतस्चेतरश्चैनं कृतान्तः परिकर्षति॥

nAtmanaH kAmakArosti purushhoyamanIshvaraH / itashcetarataschainam kRRitAntaH parikarshhati.

Man is not able to do what he wills. Fate pulls him hither and thither. Rama tells his brother Bharata to use his will power to understand the shastras and his own advice and act accordingly. Rama explains all this to Bharata in 15 shlokas in Ayodhya Kand sarga 105 starting with the above shloka. Rama emphasizes the importance of our Samayachara which is to obey father's words.

Slokas 8 to 14: To be understood and assimilated before age 40

Between the ages of 20 and 40 one should have had lessons – learnt and unlearnt - from the world that worldly conception of happiness is never the ultimate! These seven shlokas underline the concept of the real Ultimate and tell you that Bhakti is the means to get the Ultimate!

8. Chandogya Upanishad: 7-24-1: Sanatkumara to Narada:

यत्र नान्यत्-पश्यति नान्यत्-श्रृणोति नान्यद्-विजानाति स भूमा
अथ यत्र अन्यत्-पश्यति अन्यत्-श्रृणोति अन्यद्-विजानाति
तद्-अल्पं यो वै भूमा तद्-अमृतं अथ यद्-अल्पं तन्मर्त्यं

Yatra nAnyatpashyati nAnyat shRRiNoti nAnyad vijAnAti sa bhUmA. ath yatra anyat pashyati anyat shRRiNoti anyad vijAnAti tadalpaM. yo vai bhUmA tadamRitaM. atha yadalpaM tanmartyaM.

Where one sees nothing else, hears nothing else, is aware of nothing else, that is the Infinite. Where one sees something else, hears something else, is aware of something else, that is the Finite. The Infinite is immortal while the Finite is mortal. (Ch.U. 7.24.1). Since Brahman, the infinite immortal. Is the only one existing everywhere, you are not supposed to be aware of anything else ever.

9. Kapila gita in Bhagavatam: (III-27-12,13)

यथा जलस्थ आभासः स्थलस्थेना-वदृश्यते
स्वाभासेन तथा सूर्यो जलस्थेन दिवि स्थितः
एवं त्रिवृद्-अहंकारो भूतेन्द्रिय-मनोमयैः
स्वाभासैर्-लक्षितोनेन सदाभासेन सत्य-दृक्

yathA jalastha AbhAsaH sthalasthenA-vadRRishyate /
svAbhAsena tathA sUryo jalasthena divi sthitaH //
evaM trivRRid-ahaMkAro bhUtendriya-manomayaiH /
svAbhAsair-lakShito'nena sadAbhAsena satya-dRRik /

The presence of the Supreme Lord can be realized just as the sun is realized first as a reflection on water, and again as a second reflection on the wall of a room, although the sun itself is situated in the sky. The self-realized soul is thus reflected first in the threefold ego and then in the body, senses and mind. The topic is how one recognises that the Supreme is the One Power behind every action and every presence in the universe. Imagine a hall in which there is a large vessel of water that receives direct sunlight and reflects it onto the opposite wall in the hall. What is the source of this light on the wall? It is the reflected Sun in the water (contained in the vessel). And what is the source of that reflected Sun? It is the actual Sun in the blazing sky. So also we individuals seem to be having awareness of the outside world. The source of our awareness is our consciousness within. But this consciousness itself is a reflection of the real supreme Consciousness, the reflection being in our own ego-mind.

Now Kapila continues this thought process to its logical conclusion. Our mind goes to sleep when we experience dreamless sleep. In fact, all the senses of perception, cognition and action seem to have disappeared during our sleep. Where have they gone? They have all merged in our own Ignorance. That is why we are totally unaware of anything at that time. But there is the "I" part, which is not sleeping. It never sleeps. The "I" is always existing. *But it is bereft of the thought of "I"-hood*. That is, it is without egoism (*nir-aham-kriyaH*). It is in fact the only witness to everything that is happening around it. It sees everything go to sleep – the body, the senses, the mind and even the egoism. So the egoism is lost. But It itself (the "I") is not lost. *When the "I"-hood is absent it may look as though the self is dissolved. But this view is as false as thinking that a man who has been robbed of his wealth is destroyed.* (III–27–15)

मन्यमानस्-तदात्मानं अनष्टो नष्टवन्-मृषा नष्टे
अहम्करणे द्रष्टा नष्टवित्त इवातुरः

manyamAnas-tadAtmAnaM anashhTo
nashhTavan-mRRishhA / nashhTe
ahamkaraNe drashhTA nashhTavitta
ivAturaH

10. From Shankara's Shivamanasa puja

आत्मा त्वं गिरिजामतिः परिजनाः प्राणाः शरीरं गृहं
पूजा ते विषयोपभोगरचना निद्रा समाधि-स्थितिः।
सञ्चारः पदयोः प्रदक्षिणविधिः स्तोत्राणि सर्वा गिरो
यद्यत् कर्म करोमि तत्तदखिलं शम्भो तवाराधनं॥

AtmA tvaM girijAmatiH parijanAH
prANAH sharIraM gRRihaM
pUjA te vishhayopabhogaracanA nidrA
samAdhi-sthitiH.
sa~nchAraH padayoH
pradakshhiNavidhiH stotrANi sarvA giro
yadyat karma karomi tattadakhilaM
shambho tavArAdhanaM.

O Lord, You are my Atma (Soul), Devi Girija (the Divine Mother) is my Buddhi (Pure Intellect), the Shiva Ganas (the Companions or Attendants) are my Prana and my Body is Your Temple, My Interactions with the World are Your Worship and my Sleep is the State of Samadhi (complete absorption in You), My Feet Walking about is our Pradakshina (Circumambulation); all my Speech are Your Hymns of Praises, Whatever work I do, all that is Your Aradhana (Worship), O Shambhu. This is the *Atma-nivedanaM,* the last of the nine-fold methodologies enunciated by Prahlada in the Bhagavatam. It is also the complete surrender described in all bhakti literature and particularly in the Gita. The expression literally means "By the attitude which is ready to lay one's life at the Divine feet". When that attitude is present, all talk becomes a Japa, all action becomes a *mudrA* and so on. A person who can do this surrender would have his whole life sanctified as a pUjA to The Almighty.

Almost the very same set of ideas is spelt out in shloka 27 of Soundaryalahari (starting with *japo jalpaH*). It is also the complete surrender described in all bhakti literature and particularly in the Gita. The core word used is '*AtmArpana-*

dRRisha "The expression literally means "By the attitude which is ready to lay one's life at the divine feet". When that attitude is present, all talk becomes a Japa, all action becomes a *mudrA* and so on. A person who can do this surrender would have his whole life sanctified as a pUjA to the Almighty. Such a dedication of everything at the feet of the Lord is prescribed by the Gita also: "Whatever you do, whatever you consume, whatever you offer in the homa-fire, whatever you give away, whatever intense concentration you do – all that should be offered to Me" (B.G. 9-27). 'There is nothing that I do', 'Good or bad, Am I the doer?' – Such expressions of total surrender are everywhere in the works of Shaiva Nayanmars, Vaishnava Alvars and also the saints of other religions. It is this kind of total surrender that gives the destination of one's birth, namely JIvanmukti. What is talked of as 'the cessation of mind' in the path of jnAna becomes the 'total surrender' in the path of Bhakti. Both are "*AtmArpaNaM*" only. To sum up, the body does what it does because it gets the power fromthe JIva within it; so also what all this JIva does is because it gets the power from a supreme JIva-shakti behind it and that is the Mother Goddess.

For that shakti not only this JIva but all the other JIvas constitute the body; — nay, the entire Universe is the body. Once this idea settles deeply in our mental system there will be no problem of laying our lives at Her feet.

11. From Vivekachudamani

जन्तूनां नरजन्म-दुर्लभं अतः पुम्स्त्वं ततो विप्रता
तस्माद्वैदिककर्ममार्गपरता विद्वत्वमस्मात्परम्।
आत्मानात्मविवेचनं स्वनुभवो ब्रह्मात्मना संस्थितिः
मुक्तिर्नो शतकोटिजन्मसुकृतैः पुण्यैर्विना लभ्यते॥

jantUnAM narajanmadurlabhaM ataH
pumstvaM tato vipratA
tasmAdvaidika-karma-mArga-paratA
vidvatvamasmAtparaM
AtmAnAtmavivechanaM svanubhavo
brahmAtmanA samsthitiH
Muktirno shatakoTijanmasukrritaiH
puNyairvinA labhyate.

For all living ceatures, a human birth is rare; much more difficult it is to attain full manhood. Rarer is a satvic attitude. To have steadfastness on the path of spiritual activity as explained in vedic scriptures is rare; much more so to have a correct knowledge of the deep significance of scriptures. Discrimination of the Real from the unreal, a personal experience of spiritual glory and ultimately to get fully established in the living consciousness that the self in me is the self in all - these come only later on and culmination in one's liberation – Nothing of this can be had without earned merits of hundred crores of livees lived intelligently.

12. Shata-shlokI 54: Three Aspects of the supreme Self

पूर्णात्मानात्मभेदात् त्रिविधमिह परं बुध्यवच्छिन्नमन्यत्
तत्रैवाभासमात्रं गगनमिव जले त्रिप्रकारं विभाति।
अम्भोवच्छिन्नमस्मिन् प्रतिफलितमतःपाथसोऽन्तर्बहिश्च
पूर्णावच्छिन्नयोगे व्रजति लयमविद्या स्वकार्यैः सहैव॥

pUrNAtmaanAtmabhedAt trividhamiha
paraM buddhyavacchhinnam-anyat
tatraivabhAsamAtraM gaganamiva jale
triprakAraM vibhAti.
ambhovacchhinnamasmin
pratipalitamataH pAthaso.antarbahishca
pUrnAvacchinnayoge
vrajatilayamaviyasvakAryaiH sahaiva.

This Supreme Self has three aspects according to (its being) the Full (*pUrNa*), the Self (*AtmA*) and the non-self (*anAtmA*); they are

1. the unconditioned Self, US
2. that which is conditioned or delimited by the intellect: CS and
3. that which is only a reflection in the intellect; RS

just as space manifests in three ways, namely

1. the full space which is inside and outside (a vessel or a pond) US
2. that which is occupied by water (in the vessel or the pond) – which is therefore limited by the contours of the vessel or the pond and CS
3. that which is reflected in that water. RS

The jIva which is the reflection of the Ultimate in the intellect, is known as *cidAbhAsa* and is usually mistaken as the self. When it is so mistaken it is the non-self (3) of this shloka. This is the space that is reflected in water. The real self is the AtmA (the *jIvAtmA*) which is the *sAkshhI*, also sometimes called *kUTastha,* and corresponds to the space (2) inside the vessel (pond), that is hidden or covered by water. And then there is the *pUrNAtmA* or Brahman which corresponds to the space (1) everywhere including the inside of the vessel pond). Vidyaranya's Pancadashi proposes this analogy in Ch.5 starting from shloka 18 onwards.

In the Bhagavad Gita Chapter 15, almost at the end (shlokas 16 to 18) Krishna refers to three *purushhas*, namely *kshara-purushha* (Perishable purushha), *akshara Purushha* (Imperishable purushha) and Purushhottama. These correspond respectively to Nos. (3), (2) and (1) above, namely RS, CS & US

When the conditioned Self merges in (identifies with) the unconditioned, the Causal Ignorance disappears along with all its effects. The identity is that of the KUTastha with the All-pervading Brahman. When this is achieved, the JIva, a mere appearance, becomes inconsequential. The all-pervading, infinite, macro Brahman, when available at the micro level for the JIva to relate with as the witness of the mind-body complex, takes the name of Kutastha. It is the realisation that the Kutashta is indeed identical with the infinite Brahman that is spoken of as liberating knowledge that destroys Ignorance.

Another way of looking at the three purushas is the following. Whenever we say 'I' by referring to ourselves we are actually referring to the body, mind intellect. This is the ksharapurusha or RS in the above. If on the other hand we identify ourselves with the JIvAtma inside (which is basically unconnected with the body mind intellect, though it thinks so by mistake) we are talking of the Aksharapurusha.

<table>
<tr><th colspan="4">THREE ASPECTS OF THE SELF</th></tr>
<tr><th>With respect to a pot with water</th><th>With respect to BMI</th><th>With respect to the Absolute</th><th>Source of Reference</th></tr>
<tr><td>JALAKASHA
= Universal Space seen as reflection in water</td><td>CONSCIOUSNESS reflected in mind
= CHIDABHASA</td><td>Kshara Purusha
= Jiva
= BMI and Chidabhasa</td><td rowspan="3">B.G. Ch.15 shloka 16;
Panchadashi 6 – 18;
Shatashloki No.54;
Gems of Shankara p.56;
THUS SPAKE KRISHNA p.409</td></tr>
<tr><td>GHATAKASHA
= Space within the pot occupied by water</td><td>Individual Self
= aham</td><td>Akshara Purusha
= KuTastha
= Pure Consciousness</td></tr>
<tr><td>MAHAKASHA
= Universal space including the space within, outside & the pot</td><td colspan="2">BRAHMAN
= ABSOLUTE CONSCIOUSNESS
= PARAMATMAN</td></tr>
</table>

13. Narayaneeyam 91-3

भीतिर्नाम द्वितीयाद्भवति ननु मनः कल्पितं च द्वितीयं
हृदयम्-इह यथाशक्ति बुद्ध्या निरुन्ध्यां
मायाविद्धे तु तस्मिन् पुनरपि न तथा भाति मायाधि-नाथं
तत्-त्वां भक्त्या महत्या सततम्-अनुभजन्-नीश भीतिं विजह्यां

bhItirnAma dvitIyAdbhavati nanu manH
kalpitaM ca dvitIyaM
tenaikyAbhyAsashIlo hRRidayam-iha
yathAshakti buddhyA nirundhyAM /
mAyAviddhe tu tasmin punarapi na tathA
bhAti mAyAdhi-nAthaM
tat-tvAM bhaktyA mahatyA satatam-
anubhajan-nIsha bhItiM vijahyAM //

This is one of the key shlokas in Narayaneeyam that trumpets the highest advaita concept, The sentence *'manaH-kalpitam dvitIyaM'* (The consciousness of a second object is an imaginary superimposition of the mind) constitutes the 'brahma-sUtra' of advaita. Bhattatiri clearly makes the point that the unity of the JIva with the supreme Spirit is the ultimate goal. But he hastens to add that the same is not reachable by any one directly but only through the love and service of Him and His Grace. It is only by God's

Grace that non-dual consciousness is obtained. The devotee merges in His Being by His grace, The 'I' disappears in Him and 'He' is left. The becoming merges in the Being. It is not vice versa. This is what one might call Realistic *advaita*, to be subtly contrasted with '*kevala-advaita*'.

14. From Kathopanishad

सूर्यो यथा सर्वलोकस्य चक्षुः न लिप्यते चक्षुषैर्बाह्यदोषैः
एकस्तथा सर्वभूतान्तरात्मा न लिप्यते लोकदुःखेन बाह्यः ॥

sUryo yathA sarvalokasya chakshhuH na lipyate cakshhushhairbAhyadoshhaiH
ekastathA sarvabhUtAntarAtmA na lipyate lokaduHkhena bAhyaH.

Just as the Sun which is the eye of the whole world, is not tainted by the ocular and external defects, similarly the Self, that is but one, the immanent one, in all beings, is not tainted by the sorrows of the world, it being transcendental

15 to 21: To be understood and assimilated before age 60

By the time one reaches age 60 one must feel the necessity to go spiritual and adopt the relevant style of living towards that end. That is what these seven shlokas are for! They also tell you what precisely is spiritual living.

15. Shivananda lahari No.81 of Adi Shankaracharya

कञ्चित्-कालम्-उमामहेश भवतः पादारविन्दार्चनैः
कञ्चित्-ध्यान-समाधिभिश्च नतिभिः कञ्चित् कथा-कर्णनैः
कञ्चित्-कञ्चिद्-अवेक्षणैश्च नुतिभिः कञ्चिद्-दशामीदृशीं
यः प्राप्नोति मुदा त्वदर्पित-मना जीवन् स मुक्तः खलु

ka~ncit-kAlam-umAmahesha bhavataH pAdAravindArcanaiH
ka~ncit-dhyAna-samAdhibhishca natibhiH ka~ncit kathA-karNanaiH /
ka~ncit-ka~ncid-avekshhaNaishca nutibhiH ka~ncid-dashAmIdR^ishIM
yaH prApnoti mudA tvadarpita-manA jIvan sa muktaH khalu//

Meaning, Sometime in worshipping Your lotus feet, sometime in meditation and concentration sometime in offering obeisance, sometime in listening to stories about You, sometime in looking at Your form, sometime in singing Your praise - he who gains such a state in exhultation, having surrendered his mind to You, O Lord, he is verily liberated even when alive.

16. From Yajurveda – aghamarshanasUktaM:

आर्द्रम् ज्वलति ज्योतिरहमस्मि ज्योतिर्ज्वलति ब्रह्माहमस्मि।
योहमस्मि ब्रह्माहमस्मि अहमस्मि ब्रह्माहमस्मि
अहमेवाहम् माम् जुहोमि स्वाहा ॥

Ardram jvalati jyotirahamasmi
jyotirjvalati brahmAhamasmi.
yohamasmi brahmAhamasmi ahamasmi
brahmAhamasmi
ahamevAham mAm juhomi svAhA.

That Supreme Light which projected itself as the Universe like a soaked seed that sprouts (or that Supreme Light which shines as the substratum of the liquid element) – I am that Supreme Light. I am that supreme Light of brahman which shines as the innermost essence of all that exists. In reality I am the same infinite Brahman (even when I am experiencing myself as a finite self owing to my Ignorance). Now by the onset of Knowledge I am really that brahman which is my eternal nature. Therefore I realise this identity by making myself, the finite self, an oblation into the fire of the infinite brahman which I am always. May this oblation be well made.

Note the translation above of '*mAM juhomi svAhA*' as 'myself, the finite self is made as an oblation into the fire'. Every time the word '*svAhA*' word is used for an oblation into the fire, it is not to be taken as a ritualistic repetition of a word called '*svAhA*'. The word '*svAhA*' in the context of the oblation is to be taken as '*svatva-hananaM*', that is, 'the killing of the concept of the finite self'. Though ritualists may refer to '*svAhA*' as the name of the wife of Agni, the Fire-God, *it is indeed the destruction of the finite self that is required by the ritual of oblation into the fire*.

One of the beauties of Hinduism is that it teaches us that, while God is infinitely higher than ourselves, He is also infinitely near to us. He is nearer to us than our hands and feet. He is the Soul of our souls. This concept of immanence is the strongest point of Sanatana Dharma. He is the one that survives in us from childhood to adulthood and through old age, from birth, as the I that we talk of when we refer to ourselves (7th shloka of Dakshinamurthi ashtakam of Shankara). He is neither the body nor the senses, nor the mind nor the ego, nor the intellect; He is the I that is none of these, but is far distant from anything that we can call ours in a related manner like spouse, issue, wealth, possessions and so forth (1st shloka of *Advaita-pancharatnam* of Shankara). He is the ever-present witness to all our experiences. He is really our Atman. He is Brahman. He is the One Reality beyond which there is none. Brahman and Atman differ, if at all, only in our approach. Atman is the name given to the highest Reality if we seek one such within ourselves. Brahman is the name given to the highest Reality if we seek one such in the universe. The greatest revelation of the Upanishads is the essential identity between Brahman (also denoted by the word paramAtman) and Atman (also known by the word jIvAtman, or the soul) as revealed by the grand mystic pronouncements called the *mahAvAkyas* of the four Vedas. Once the identity is established, the two terms become interchangeable and it makes no difference whether we speak of the Absolute of the Upanishads as Brahman or Atman. This Absolute is the three-fold reality, namely sat (Existence), cit (Consiousness) and Bliss (Ananda).

But even though Godhead is so near to all of us, it is very difficult to realise Him. This is because we have to cease to be ourselves before we can know Him as He is. The difficulty in this concept is the fact that God is both transcendent and immanent. The immanence aspect is inbuilt into the concept of Atman and the transcendence aspect in the concept of Brahman. The scriptures, particularly the Upanishads and the Gita share with us their dilemma in having to describe both these aspects simultaneously. They adopt one of two alternatives. On the one hand they use the superlatives of all the qualities they can think of: it is smaller than the smallest, bigger than the biggest, it is that which is supreme, than which there is nothing higher, than which there is nothing more minute, than which there is nothing more comprehensive (M.N.U)).

He strides the entire universe, He is the purest of the pure, most auspicious of all that is auspicious, the God of Gods, the Imperishable Father of all Beings. (Preliminary shlokas to V.S.).

On the other hand they use negation of all the finite things that we are capable of expressing: whatever cannot be indicated by speech but that motivates all speech, that is Brahman; whatever cannot be seen by the eyes, but by which the eye sees, that is Brahman; not that which is worshipped (Kenopanishad);

neither internal consciousness nor external consciousness nor both; not a bundle of consciousness either; not the conscious One nor the non-conscious One; cannot be perceived, cannot be related, cannot be handled, cannot be attributed, cannot be indicated, nor can it be an object of thought (M.U.)

When the scriptures use negatives like these we should not take them to mean that Brahman is just a complete negation. It only means that our finite expressions can never do full justice to the infinite grandeur that is God, that God is wholly other than what we know in the world. He is the unifying principle behind all creatures. He is the canvas on which we shine as painted pictures.

Resuming our earlier three-fold presentation of Reality, as *sat*, *cit* and *Ananda* we have to note that it is also reflected in the most important *mantra* of Hinduism, namely, the *GAyatrI*. The three lines of the *GAyatrI* mean, literally:

That – of the Originator – Most excellent; Light – of God – Let us meditate; Intellects – He who – Our – May prompt.

तत्-सवितुर्वरेण्यं
भर्गो-देवस्य धीमहि
धियो-यो नः प्रचोदयात्

tat-saviturvareNyaM;
bhargo-devasya dhImahi;
dhiyo-yo naH pracodayAt

The word *savituH* in **the first line**, which indicates 'Origin' or 'Birth', suggests Creation and makes it characteristic of the '*sat*' or the '*satya*' facet of the Absolute Reality. This line is a *glorification of the Absolute*. A glorification of a deity simply praises the Lord as Lord, does not ask for anything and does not do anything in the wake of that praise. It is like a subordinate visiting his superior (or a party worker visiting his leader) purely for courtesy and simply offering words of praise without expecting anything to be done by the superior. The first line of the *GAyatrI* does simply this. **The second line** asks us to meditate as if it is the be-all and end-all of life. Yes, because the meditation itself gives the bliss, immanent in the Absolute Reality. Meditation on the Absolute is communion with or worship of, the Divine. It is therefore the *worship aspect* of the *mantra*. It corresponds to the *Ananda* (or the *ananta*, infinite) aspect of the Absolute; because the very meditation of the Absolute is Bliss. Bliss is not something that you attain after you have achieved something as a reward from the Lord. To think of Him is Bliss! The use of the words *dhiyah* and *pracodayAt* in **the third line** show that this line is indicative of the *cit* facet of Reality and is also the *Prayer aspect* of the *mantra* imbedded in the *GAyatrI*. It is the *cit* (Knowledge, *jnAnaM*) facet of the *sat-cid-Ananda* form or the *satyam-jnAnaM-anantam* definition of *Brahman*. It is significant that in this line it is the intellect that asks for the prompting of the Absolute and that is why this line is the *cit* facet. A deeper enquiry into the meaning of the *mantra* will take us into the analysis of the state of sleep and our memory of it. In fact the *sat-cid-Ananda* form is our true nature, though we don't know it. But every day when we go to sleep and come back with the memory of a happy sleep, it is because we have gone and touched that true nature of us without our own volition. Thus the three lines together, of the *GAyatrI* incorporate, in a sense, the three-fold universal practice of all Religion, namely, **Glorification of the**

super-natural, Worship of the Supra-mental and Prayer to The All-mighty. The three lines represent the three different types of propitiation of the Absolute. All the different connotations of the *GAyatrI* may now be summarised in a Table as below:

'tat savituH …'	Glorification (or Creation)	I	ahaM	Experience	sat
'bhargo …'	Communion (or Merging)	happily	sukhaM	Happiness	Ananda
'*dhiyo* ….'	Prayer (or Realisation)	slept	asvApsaM	Awareness	cit

17. From Bhagavatam: Dhruva-stuti

त्वं नित्य-मुक्त-परिशुद्ध-विबुद्ध आत्मा
कूतस्थ आदि-पुरुषो भगवान्-स्त्र्यधीशः
यद्-बुद्ध्य्-अवस्थितिम्-अखण्डितया स्वदृष्ट्या
द्रष्टा स्थिता-वधिमखो व्यतिरिक्त आस्से

tvaM nitya-mukta-pariSuddha-
vibuddha AtmA
kUtastha Adi-purusho bhagavAn-
stryadhISaH/
yad-buddhy-avasthitim-akhaNDitayA
svadRshTyA
drashTA sthitA-vadhimakho
vyatirikta Asse//

You are ever-liberated, perfectly pure, the Omniscient Self, the Immutable, the most Ancient Person, the One with all divine attributes, the Lord of the three worlds and guNas. You, though being the uninterrupted Witness, by your Cosmic Vision, of the state of intelligence and also the Lord of all sacrifices, are ever aloof from the JIva, the individual soul.

This shloka and Arjuna's two shlokas (Ch.11, B.G. shlokas 18 & 38) have a common characteristic. Namely, though a form of God is standing before them they worship it with words describing a Nirguna brahman.

God is the support for the universe. What does this mean? It does not mean that God is lifting the Universe on His head or shoulders. Let us take two examples for understanding what 'support' means here. All of us have seen the ocean and its waves. Now what is the 'support' for the waves? The physical support is of course the ocean. But there is something more that is meant here. Without the ocean, waves cannot exist. Waves exist because of the ocean. It is in this sense that God is the support for us and the universe. Without God, we or the universe cannot exist.

This is what is meant by 'You are the ultimate support for the entire universe'.

Second example. We have all seen movies. Movies are seen on the screen. Without a screen, there cannot be any movies. The screen may be a real cloth screen or maybe a computer screen or a cell phone screen. But a screen has to be there for the movies to exist and be seen. God is the screen. We and the universe are all movies on that God-screen. Without the God-screen none of us or the universe can exist. So just as the screen is the ultimate support for the movies, God is the ultimate support for the entire universe.

In fact #s *18 & 38* of B.G ch.11 are magnificent spiritual eulogies, probably unparallelled in their content as well as in their simplicity, in any religious literature of the world, other than the Upanishads and Itihasa-purAnas.

You are the most ancient Lord (*tvam-AdidevaH*), the primal Spirit (*purushhaH purANaH*), the supreme abode of this universe (*asya vishvasya paraM nidhAnaM*). You are the Knower (*vettA asi*) and also whatever is to be known (*vedyaM ca*), You are the Ultimate Transcendental One (*paraM ca dhAma*); Oh Being of Infinite forms, (*anantarUpa)*, You pervade the entire universe (*tvayA tatam vishvaM*).

Here the mention about infinite forms needs some explanation. '*anantarUpa'* means Infinite number of forms. This is one of the most fundamental, but also the most misunderstood truths, of Hinduism. God is only one. There is no second opinion throughout the Hindu religion. But that One Absolute God, appears and manifests in multifarious forms. He is Vishnu, He is Shiva, He is Vinayaka, He is Su*brahman*ya, He is the same one who appears also in female forms like Lakshmi, Parvati, Saraswati, etc. Some people ind it difficult to understand this truth of Hinduism. They ask 'Why do you have so many Gods?' How can there be so many Gods? And so forth. A good answer was once given by Kanchi Maha Periava. Suppose you had in your photo album, photos of your father, one in his office dress, one in his swimming suit, one in his pyjamas, one in his *dhoti* worn in a traditional orthodox way, one in his shorts, which he wears when he is gardening, and one in a female dress in which he was acting in a drama... and so on in several dresses. Your friend visits you and sees this album. You tell him: All these are my father's photos. Suppose he asks you: 'Do you have so many fathers? '. Is it not a totally absurd question? So also is the question 'Do you have so many gods?'- There is only one God Absolute. For various purposes He appears in various forms. Not only the well-known forms of Vishnu and Shiva. He appears sometimes as a man-lion, sometimes as an ordinary man, sometimes as a hunter, sometimes as a boar or a pig or a fish, each time there is a purpose. That is why Arjuna says in this *shloka 'tvayA tatam vishvam Ananta-rupa'*. Hey, God with infinite forms, You have pervaded this entire world. In fact it has more meanings. Whatever you see in the world, - a tree, a mountain, an animal, anything, it is all God's manifestation only. This is the greatness of Hindu religion. God is in everything, more, Everything is God. Even more, there is nothing else but God!

Another important fact from this *shloka* is: knower and the known are both God. In fact, everything is God. Subject and object are both God. The seer (one who sees) and the seen are both God. The One God manifests as everything.

Further there is a vedantic deeper insight here. The Supreme is the *VettA*, therefore the intelligent cause (*nimitta-kAraNaM*) for all creation; but He is also the *paraM nidhAnaM*, namely the supreme basis, therefore He is also the material cause (*upAdAna kAraNaM*).

We see millions of objects in the universe, including our own human beings and other living beings. Just as we human beings, each of us wihout exception, have an immanent presence of the absolute brahman in us, the universe of objects also has this immanent presence. Immanence is the word. This word has generally no importance for other religions, because they do not think of their god without form or attributes. Even the deities in our temples have the immanent presence of the absolute brahman. Whatever you see is Brahman in its immanent presence in the object you see. The object you see, including the universe, is only mAyA. This mAyA is the shakti of Brahman and it is what expresses itself as everything in the world, including the objects you, including the saguna brahman you worship. The effect of mAya is, what you see is not absolutely real, it is only an experience and nothing more — like the movie we see on a screen.

There are two important words often occurring in Vedanta. One is the word 'transcendental' and the other is the word 'transactional'. The absolute Brahman (Nirguna brahman) is the transcendental truth whereas the universe within which we operate is only a transactional (operational) truth. The transactional truth ultimately turns out to be no truth at all, because it disappears. The transactional truth is like the roles that the same actor appears in different TV serials. In one serial he may be the husband of an actress and in another serial he may be the brother of the same actress playing a different role. Any one who confuses the transactional and the transcendental truths will have to go a long way. He is the one who comes out with the question: If you say there is only one absolute God, then why do you go and worship different Gods in temples? Mixing up of the transactional and transcendental truth is the problem. These are the people who ask you: Which is greater? Saguna brahman or Nirguna brahman? Saguna brahman is the voluntary show-off of mAyA.

Even within it there is the immanent presence of Nirguna-brahman. Each transactional object in the world, whether it is a material object or whether it is a divine deity should be understood to have the transcendental truth immanent in it, inspite of the outer visibility. This is the beauty of the concept of immanence.

Yacca kimcijjagat sarvam dRRishyate shrUte.pi va / antar-bahishca tatsarvaM vyApya nArAyana sthitah –

says the Mahanarayanopanishad. So in every object we should be able to see the godly presence. That is why when we say namaste to others, we must remember it is actually addressed to the immanent absolute embedded in the other person just as the immanent presence of the Self in us.

The significance of this stuti by Dhruva is that the is looking at the form of Vishnu standing before him but still he is not confused that it is the same transcendental concept of Nirguna brahman which shows before him with a form! And it is the same with Arjuna's shlokas!

18. From Yajurveda's adaptation of NasadIyasUkta of Rigveda

को अद्धा वेद क इह प्रवोचत् कुत आजाता कुत इयम् विसृष्टिः
अर्वाग् देवा अस्य विसर्जने न अथा को वेद यत आबभूव
इयम् विसृष्टिर्-यत आबभूव यदि वादधे यदि वा न
यो अस्या-ध्यक्षः परमे व्योमन् सो अङ्ग वेद यदि वा न वेद

ko addhA veda ka iha pravocat / kuta
AjAtA kuta iyam visRRishhTiH //
arvAg devA asya visarjane na / athA ko
veda yata AbabhUva //
iyam visRRishhTir-yata AbabhUva / yadi
vAdadhe yadi vA na //
yo asyA-dhyakshhaH parame vyoman / so
a~Nga veda yadi vA na veda //

Who verily knows and who can declare it? Whence it was born, and whence this manifold creation sprang? The lower gods who came later into being would not know. Does the Creator, from whom everything came, know? Does He know whether it was His will or not that formed it? The topmost Seer that is in highest heaven, He verily knows it — or perchance He knows not.

19. Panchadashi 6-128

युक्तिदृष्ट्या त्वनिर्वाच्यं नासदासीदिति श्रुतेः।
नासदासित् विभातत्वात् नोसदासीच्च बाधनात्॥

yuktidRRishhTyA tvanirvAcyaM nAsadAsIditi shruteH. nAsadAsit vibhAtatvAt nosadAsIcca bAdhanAt.

By human logic it is undecidable. The *nAsadIya sUkta* also says so. Originally it could not have been non-existence, because now it exists; it could not have been Existence, because the universe came into being later and that means whatever that existed has changed.

20. Shruti Gita in Bhagavatam (X-87-15)

बृहद्-उपलब्दम्-एतद्-अवयन्त्यवशेषतया
यत उदयास्तमयौ विकृतेर्मृद्-इवा-विकृतात्।
अत ऋषयो दधुस्-त्वयि मनो-वचना-चरितं
कथम्-अयथा भवन्ति भुवि दत्त-पदानि नृणां॥

bRRihad-upalabdam-etad-avayantyavasheshhatayA yata udayAstamayau vikRRitermRRid-ivA-vikRRitAt.

ata RRishhayo dadhus-tvayi mano-
vacanA-caritaM
katham-ayathA bhavanti bhuvi datta-
padAni nRRiNAM.

The wise recognize this Universe to be Brahman, because it is Brahman that is the residual. It is from and into Brahman that the universe emanates and dissolves - just as from earth earthenware rise and fall. Therefore when we glorify any God by words contemplated by the mind, and names spoken by the tongue the praise has to go only to you. Placing one's foot on a mountain does not mean that one is keeping his feet not on Earth.[1]

etat upalabdhaM bRhat:- This visible universe is *Brahman*

mano-vacanA-caritaM:- executed by the mind and the speech.

ayathA:- not (placed) on Earth.

vacana-AcaritaM (the essence of Vedanta) *tvayi* (is in you)

mano dadhuH (fixed their mind) (*tvayi* = in your Ultimate Form).

It is *Brahman* that is the residual after everything is gone. So the Cause is to be known, not the effect.

Knowing the cause, we know everything that has to be known. Before manifestation, and after dissolution, whatever is existent is the Absolute Truth. The vedas in their text talk of different Gods, but these are only names and forms. All of them ultimately go only to the Permanent Absolute.

The beautiful analogy of the step on the mountain being the same as a step on Earth, is cited here. This analogy, to my limited knowledge, appears to be available nowhere else in the vast scriptural literature of Hinduism. That shows the originality of the vedas; they don't repeat what everybody else says; they have their own original way of expression! This verse by itself is enough to quell the doubting critic of the vedas, in connection with the mention, in the vedas, of the various gods, *agni, varuna, vayu, soma, surya, indra,* etc. The criticism is usually of the following kind. Throughout the vedic literature one finds that sometimes it is *varuNa*, the Divinity representing Water, sometimes it is *agni,* the fire-God and some other times it is *indra* the Lord of the divines that are eulogised with superlatives. For instance, when the earliest western readers came across vedic statements like *agnir-mUrdhA divaH* (Fire-God is the King of the Divine World), *sUrya AtmA jagatas-tasthushaSca* (The Sun-God is the soul of the mobile as well as the immobile) *indro yAto'vasitasya rAjA* (Indra is the King of the mobile and the immobile), *Apo vA idam sarvaM* (Water is this Universe) they propounded the thought process that during the vedic times it was all pantheism or polytheism and only later, almost at the end of the first millenium B.C.E. that the One God idea came up. This thought process may be a welcome line of research for occidental thinking. But if you look at the superlatives being used in the same manner and language for each vedic deity one cannot but conclude that the last words are those passages where each such deity is considered as only one expression of the many-faceted supreme Almighty. And here is the verse in the *Shruti Gita* which should put an end to such wild speculations of the uninformed reader.

21. From Vaidyanatha - ashtakam

वेदान्त-वेद्याय जगन्-मयाय योगीश्वर-ध्येय-पदाम्भुजाय
त्रिमूर्ति-रूपाय सहस्त्र-नाम्ने श्री वैद्यनाथाय नमः शिवाय

vedAntavedyAya jaganmayAya
yogishvara-dhyeya padAmbhujAya.
trimUrtirUpAya sahasranAmne shrI
vaidyanAthAya namaH shivAya.

This is a Vedantic shloka embedded in an 8-shloka hymn, which is otherwise, a very common type of prayer, particularly oriented towards the Vaidyanatha deity (the Lord of all doctors and doctoring) of a temple near Chidambaram. This verse contains a mine of Vedantic import. First of all the 'namaH shivAya' mantra is imbedded in it. The five (impersonal) epithets that govern the name of the Absolute indicate the only five ultimates to which everything may be reduced, namely, sat, cit, Ananda, nAma and rUpa, as a penultimate step to the final reduction to the advaitic One and Only One. The first is the 'sat' aspect, the 'I' that transcends everything. That transcendent entity is the essential common content of That as well as This. Any attempt to know It has to be done only through the teaching of Vedanta by the Guru. It is the Ultimate Knowledge that Vedanta directs you to. The next one is the 'cit' aspect. The perceptibility of the universe however is only a transitory phenomenon. Its transitoriness is exactly what makes it less real than the substratum of brahman on which it is superimposed. This is where we go to the next epithet: *jagan-mayAya.* The universe is full of Him. It is He that shows Himself as the universe. So learn to see Him in the universe. 'He who sees only the elephant in the wooden elephant is only a child in the spiritual plane. The world appears; but it only appears. Also what we see as the universe is not a transformation of brahman like what was milk earlier is now the curd that we see and taste. brahman never undergoes any change. It is brahman itself that is appearing as the universe; the rope appearing as the snake.

tri-mUrti-rUpAya: The Lord is in three forms The Vedantic tenor of this shloka reminds us that it is not just the conventional meaning of tri-mUrti that is implied here but an esoteric interpretation of everything that is three-fold.

Sahasra-nAmne: The thousand names that try to describe Him do not complete the delineation; because it can never be completed. The word 'sahasra' only indicates the non-enumerability of His names and qualities. He actually has no name and that is why any name fits Him! Each name says something about the Absolute. Since there are infinite things to say about the Absolute, the count of names is endless

In the sense of Vedanta, there are only five things: Transcendence, Immanence, Perfection, Names and forms. The first three (described in the first line of the shloka) are absolute and the last two (of the second line of the shloka) are ephemeral. The twin concepts of transcendence and immanence are unique to Sanatana dharma. Generally religions are satisfied with the concept of transcendence alone, because they think the Almighty is beyond us somewhere. The fact that He is immanent in whatever we see or use and in fact He is in us is the peculiarity of Sanatana Dharma. The Tamil tradition speaks of the almighty as '*kaDa-vul'* – meaning: '*kada*' = kadanthu, that is transcending everything ; and '*uL'* meaning, also 'inside' everything – thus incorporating both the concepts of transcendence and immanence. This is exactly what the fundamental stotra V.S. in Sanskrit begins with: *vishvam vishnuH*. Here *vishvam* meaning universe incorporates the immanent presence of the Almighty in everything that we see. And *vishnuH* signifies the transcending nature of the Almighty—He is beyond everything!

Shlokas 22 to 27 to be assimilated before age 80

These final seven shlokas tell you how a realized soul lives. This shall indeed constitute our goal.

22. From shankara's advaita-pancharatnam

नाहं देहो नेन्द्रियाण्यन्तरङ्गो नाहङ्कारः प्राणवर्गो न बुद्धिः।
दारापत्य-क्षेत्रवित्तादि दूरः साक्षी नित्यः प्रत्यगात्मा शिवोऽहम्॥

nAhaM deho nendriyAnyantarango
nAhamkAraH prANavargo na buddhiH.
dArApatya-kshhetravittAdi dUraH
sAkshhI nityaH pratyagAtmA shivo.ahaM.

I am not the body, nor the senses, nor the intellect, neither the ego nor anything of the pranas as well as the mind. I am far far removed from wife, chidren, property and money; I am just the witness as the inner resident shiva.

The *advaita* Vedanta has this to say on *sat-cidAnanda*. When a man wakes from deep sleep it is natural for him to exclaim: I slept happily. Who is this 'I' that slept happily? It is not the mind, because it was not active at the time when the 'I' was sleeping. It is not the one that recalls the happiness of the sleep, because it did not experience the happiness. Only the experiencer can recall the experience. The experiencer is the 'I'. Actually the experiencer is the lower 'I', the false 'I'. The real 'I', i.e., the higher 'I', simply watches the experience of the lower 'I'. The real 'I' is the Immutable Reality. It does not go through any change or experience. But it always 'watches'. It is the '*sAkshI*'. It is the *sat-cidAnanda* Reality. The lower 'I' goes and 'touches' it, as it were, during deep sleep and this is an everyday experience for the lower 'I'. That is why it is able to say 'I slept happily', after every awakening from deep sleep. Here there are three assertions made, all rolled into one. The word 'happily' indicates there is an *Ananda* (pleasure, happiness, joy) which was experienced during sleep; it is actually a recall of the association with the Ananda of the real 'I'. The word 'I' indicates the continuity of existence between the state of sleep and the state of waking. The word 'slept' indicates an awareness or the knowledge (= *cit*) of sleep, the awareness belonging to the witness to the sleep, namely, the real 'I'. In dreamless sleep were we conscious or not.? We feel we were not conscious. **But that is a feeling we have *after* waking from sleep**. We do not do so in sleep itself. That in us which now feels that in sleep we were not conscious is our mind. It was not present in our sleep and so it is natural for it to be ignorant of the consciousness there was in sleep. Not having experienced sleep it is unable to remember what it was like and makes mistakes about it. The state of deep sleep is beyond the mind. Consciousness was present then as consciousness. It is because of that consciousness we are able to say that we were not aware of anything then. In a dark room we are not able to see anything but still we have the awareness that we are not able to see anything; for this awareness no external light is necessary.

In the above paragraph we referred to the fact that the real 'I' is the Immutable Reality.. In the Upanishads there are four *mahAvAkyas,* — four 'grand pronouncements' — one each from each of the four Vedas. These pronouncements are very profound and strike at the root of all Vedantic knowledge. Relevant to our present context we shall take one of them here: '*ahaM brahma asmi*'. This *mahAvAkya* occurs in Br.U. (I–4–10) which belongs to the yajur veda. It means 'I am brahman', thus expressing an identity between the real 'I' within the individual and the Supreme Transcendental Brahman, that is usually known by the name of 'The Universal Self'. One of the beauties of the Upanishads is to remind us again and again that while God is infinitely higher than ourselves He is also infinitely near to us. He is the soul of our souls. He is the 'I' that is neither the body nor the senses, nor the mind nor the ego, nor the intellect. He is really our Self or Atman. Atman is the name given to the innermost reality in ourselves and *Brahman* is the utmost reality behind the universe. The revelation '*ahaM brahma asmi*' says there are no two things, 'I' and '*Brahman*'; there is only one. I am that One – I am *brahman*. (In a lighter vein, it can be said that of the only two syllables in the word 'ahaM', 'a' is the first letter of the alphabet and 'ha' the final letter of the alphabet and so 'ahaM' encompasses the entire sweep of all possible words. It is like saying 'A to Z' in the English language. So 'ahaM' represents everything and is therefore brahman!)

Among the four *mahAvAkyas* this one is born out of self-experience and so it is the *anubhava-mahA-vAkya*. However it is very difficult to realize this truth, because we have to cease to be our lower ordinary self, before we can realize this identity for ourselves. That is why many of the daily obligations that are enjoined on us aim to drive home into our system this truism. For instance, there is what is called the '*aghamarshaNa-sUktam*' which we have seen already

23. B.G. 6-32

आत्मौपम्येन सर्वत्र समं पश्यति योऽर्जुन।
सुखं वा यदि वा दुःखं स योगी परमो मतः।

Atmaupamyena sarvatra samaM
pashyatiyorjuna /
sukhaM vA yadi vA duHkhaM sa yogI
parmo mataH //

He who sees with equality (*yaH samaM pashyati*) everything in the image of one's own self (*Atmaupamyena sarvatra*) whether it be pleasure or pain (*sukhaM vA yadi*

vA duHkhaM), him I consider to be the supreme Yogi (sa yogi paramo mataH). The words are simple. The meaning is profound. This shloka has several messages to convey to us. First it is a description of how a brahma-jnAni or JIvan-mukta lives. It focusses on three great attributes of an enlightened yogi, namely, tattvajnAnaM (Knowledge of Reality), *mano-nAshaH* (elimination of the undisciplined working of the mind) and *vAsana-kshhayaH* (|dissipation of all vAsanAs). These three are the characteristics of a JIvanmukta, — so says yoga–VashishhTaM. *Tattva-jnAna* is the Knowledge that all this aggregate of dualities and multiplicities is certainly false, since it is imagined through mAyA on the nondual Self which is Consciousness-cum-Bliss. The second characteristic is mano-nAsha. Mind is a continuous flame of a lamp which keeps on undergoing transformations by a continuous flow of modifications called *vRRittis.* It is called manas because it consists of nothing but thoughts (the Sanskrit root 'man' means 'to think'). Its elimination (*nAsha)* means its culmination in the state of nirodha (restraint) of all modifications. The tendency in the mind which causes modifications like anger etc. is called *vAsanA*, because it lies embedded (*vasati*) in the mind due to past habits. Its dissipation (*kshhaya*) means non-emergence of the emotions like anger even in the presence of external stimuli. If all the vAsanAs are thus dissipated, that is *vAsanA-kshhaya.* These three are mutually dependent, says yogavAshishhtaM. When the Knowledge of Reality has arisen, no more modifications can spark in the mind; for, as an example, consider the ordinary state of man's mind. No modifications of the mind take place when unreal things like hare's horn are spoken of or referred. That is because there is no question of any external cause disturbing the mind when you speak about a hare's horn. And for the same reason, for the enlightened yogi, who is convinced of the unreality of what is seen, no mental modifications will arise because of the external impulses. Also any modification of the mind, if at all, after the onset of Realisation, is purposeless. So mind gets eliminated like fire without fuel. When mind gets eliminated there is no perception of external causes that arouse the tendencies of the mind and so *vAsanAs* get eliminated. And this makes emotions like anger, etc., impossible for the causes in the form of the vAsanAs are not there.

In fact one can experience the elimination of the mind when does meditation or nididhyasana seriously. The meditation might have started with a mantra repetition. But at one stage you try to increase the interval between the mantra repetitions. The silence between two manta repetitions is actually the experience of the Self!

24. From Kulasekhara Azhvar's Mukundamala

कृष्ण-त्वदीय-पद-पङ्कज-पञ्जरान्तं अद्यैव मे
विशतु मानस-राज-हम्सः ।
प्राण-प्रयाणसमये कफ-वाद-पित्थैः
कण्ठावरोधन-विधौ स्मरणं कुतस्ते ॥

Krishna tvadiya-pada-pankaja-
panjarantam adyaiva me visatu manasa-
raja-hamsah
PrAna-prayana-samaye kapha-vata-
pittaih Kanthavarodhana-vidhau
smaranam kutas te

Krishna, Allow my mind which is like a royal swan to enter within your feet which are like lotus stems When the soul is ready to depart, And when bile air and phlegm, choke my throat, how will I ever remember your holy name?

These immortal verses were composed by a prince of the Chera dynasty called Kulashekara Azhwar (Called Kula Shekara Perumal in Kerala). He was also called Mudaliyandan Nambi. He was one of the 12 Azhwars. The devotion to God expressed in these verses is perhaps unparalleled in any world literature.

25. From Gangashtakam of Adi Shankaracharya

मातर्जाह्नवि शम्भुसङ्गवलिते मौळौ निधायाञ्जलिम्
त्वत्तीरे वपुषोवसानसमये नारायणाङ्घ्रिद्वयम्।
सानन्दं स्मरतो भविष्यति मम प्राणप्रयाणोत्सवे
भूयाद्भक्तिरविच्युता हरिहराद्वैतात्मिका शाश्वती॥

mAtarjAhnavi shambhusangavalite
maulau nidhAyAnjalim
tvattIre vapushhovasAnasamaye
nArAyaNAngridvayaM.
sAnandaM smaratobhavishhyati mama
prANaprayANotsave
bhUyAdbhaktiravichyutAhariharAdvait
AtmikA shAshvatI

Hey mother Jahnavi, at the end of my wanderings devoted for search

For the company of lord Shiva, the end celebration of my travel of the soul,

Would happen in your bank, while I would be meditating,

Holding my two hands in salute over my head,

With happiness, on the lotus feet of Lord Vishnu.

Let my devotion to Vishnu and Shiva be non-dual and permanent,

Oh Goddess.

It is a common Hindu tradition continuing in every period of time to keep praying to God that one should breathe one's last in conscious memory of God and His name. The tradition goes back to Sage Suka's words meted out to King Parikshit, as narrated in Vyasa's Bhagavatam (2-1-6): *janmalAbhaH paraH pumsAM ante nArAyaNa-smRRitiH,* meaning: the remembrance of Narayana at the last moment of one's life is the supreme reward of human birth.

Shankara naturally belongs to this tradition. But his is an advaita-bhakti. Love of God maturing into the insight of seeing all forms and names of God as belonging to the same one Absolute and the entire universe as the manifestation of that One is advaita-bhakti. That the Acharya Shankara had this kind of bhakti is beyond question but in his characteristic style of humility he pleads with Mother Ganga to bestow on him this non-dual devotion when he remembers the Lord at the last moment of his life.

26. From NirvanashaTkam of Shankara.

अहं निर्विकल्पो निराकार-रूपो विभुत्वाच्च सर्वत्र सर्वेन्द्रियाणाम्।
नचासङ्गतं नैव मुक्तिर्न बन्धः चिदानन्दरूपः शिवोऽहं शिवोऽहं ।।

ahaM nirvikalpo nirAkArarUpo
vibhutvAcca sarvatra sarvendriyANAM
nacAsangataM naiva muktir na bandhaH
cidAnandarUpaH shivo.ahaM shivo.ahaM

I am devoid of duality, my form is formlessness, I am omnipresent, I exist everywhere, pervading all senses, I am neither attached, neither free nor limited, I am the form of consciousness and bliss, I am Shiva (that which is not)

27. From Goswami Tulsidas's Hanuman Chalisa

तुम्हरे भजन राम को पावै। जनम जनम के दुख बिसरावै॥
अंत काल रघुबर पुर जाइ जहाँ जन्म हरिभक्त कहाइ॥

tumhare bhajan rAm ko pAvai. janma
janma ke dukh bisrAvai.
ant kAl raghubar pur jAi jahA janma
haribhakt kahAi.

Singing your name gets us Rama himself and removes the sufferings of many lives. He who sings of you, at the end of the life he attains to

Lord Rama's abode where he will be born as a Devotee of Lord Rama"

Note the famous line from Sage Shuka's teaching of Bhagavatam to King Parikshit: (Bhagavatam II-1-6).

एतावान् साङ्ख्ययोगाभ्यां स्वधर्मपरिनिष्ठया।
जन्मलाभः परः पुंसां अन्ते नारायण-स्मृतिः ॥

*etAvvAn sAnkhy-yogAbhyAM svadharma-
parinishhTayA /
janmalAbhaH paraH pumsAM ante
nArAyaNasmRRitiH //*

meaning, To be put in mind of Sri Narayana at the last moment of one's life that alone is the supreme reward of human birth, howsoever this may be earned through Self-Knowledge or Devotion or even through steadfastness to one's sacred duty.

Aum tat sat

PART 2

BITS OF HEARD WISDOM

This is a very humble collection of what are intended to be summaries of the wonderful miscellany of the sixty or so talks in the Global Festival of Oneness 2021 (GFO-2021) organized by Advaita Academy in honour of the memory of *Ācārya Bhagavatpāda Śaṅkara* from May 17, 2021 to June 16 2021. I would appreciate and recommend it to those readers who are not well versed in *Vedānta* to read these 'Bits Of Heard Wisdom' several times to get a good understanding of *Vedānta*. Let me apologise to the knowledgeable readers for the errors in presentations (I hope they are only a few!) where my grasp of the subject-matter has been incorrect.

May I also crave the pardon of those *Ācāryas* and scholars whose talks have not been included in these 'BITS'? Not all talks have been summarised for the apparent reason of physical inability, but more because of my own non-comprehension of the contents of those talks.

Section A

Works of Adi Sankaracarya

Ānanda Mīmāṃsā of Taittirīyopaniṣadbhāṣya

Speaker: Swamini Satyavratananda

A short meaning of *'ānanda'* in Sanskrit is Happiness. *Mīmāṃsā* means a 'reverential analysis'. The central topic is *Brahmānanda.* Happiness could be of three kinds: First is worldly. The second is a natural one. The third is non-experiential. How can there be non-experiential happiness? That is exactly the point of enquiry now. The crux of the enquiry is you are the experiencer. How to understand that *brahmānanda* is non-experiential?

Viṣayānanda (the happiness that comes out of *'viṣaya'*, sense-objects) is what we experience. But that is only a reflection of the Ultimate *Brahmānanda. Vedānta* says no object is capable of giving *ānanda*, because if that was so, the same object should give happiness to everyone else all the time. But this is not so. But we seem to think otherwise because of our Ignorance. We think that when we get what we want in terms of our desire, there is happiness. This is because, when we want it there is a turbulence and anxiety in the mind and when we get our object the mind becomes calm and we think this is happiness; this is only a millionth microscopic reflection (*mātrā* *i*n sanskrit) of the real *Brahmānanda. Vedānta* gives a beautiful analogy. When a dog bites a dry bone, it mistakes the blood coming out of its own teeth as the juice of the *'māmsa'* that it is biting. Vedānta says that we also mistake this happiness of the *asthi* (=bone) as a happiness from a sense object.

The *Upaniṣad* takes you to the understanding of various higher and higher levels of experiential *ānanda*, by starting from the lowest level. A noble, virtuous, educated man has a certain happiness of fulfilment in the material world with all his material riches. Take that as one unit of happiness. Hundred times that is the next level of happiness, called the happiness of *manuṣya-gandharva.* Hundred times that is the next level of happiness, that of '*deva-gandharva*'. All this is experiential happiness. Like this the Upaniṣad takes you to ten higher levels: (Just a few examples of these names: *karma-devas, devas, Indra, Brihaspati, Prajapati*) On the whole there are ten levels up to the *ānanda* of *hiraṇyagarbha* – whose *ānanda* is therefore one followed by thousand zeros times the *ānanda* of the lowest unit of man's material experiential happiness with which we started. At each higher level, that happiness is also equated to the happiness of a '*śrotriya*' (a man of scriptural learning) who is in addition, an '*akāmahata*' (who is not affected by any desire). This '*akāmahata*' is the crowing component of this *ānanda mīmāṃsā* of the *Upaniṣad*. For the '*akāmahata*' is a non-*kāmahata,* meaning, his desires are absent or are vanquished. So he has a tremendous dispassion or detachment. So when the happiness levels are taken to each of the higher ten levels, each time the intensity of *vairāgya* (detachment and dispassion) increases hundred fold. It is this peak of the highest intensity of *vairāgya* that takes you to the last one which is *brahmānanda*– where you are yourself, it is non-experiential. In fact every sense-pleasure in the material world gives you only sorrow or disgust or detachment at the end of that happiness. So *vairāgya* increases. This is the graphic description of the various *ānandas* that are given in the *Upaniṣad*. The lesson is: Don't go for *Viṣayānanda* (happiness from sense objects).

In sleep or *samādhi* we seem to get 'total' *ānanda*. But when we come back from sleep there is no duality of dreamer and dream and when we come back from *samādhi* there is no triputi of the knower, known and knowledge. Yoga also takes you to an *ānanda* which is called *santoṣa* by *Patañjali*.

But all these are only 'states' (*avasthās)*. In the state of *jāgrat* (waking), by the upadeṣa of *śāstra* and guru we get the upadeṣa of 'I am *Brahman*' and that is the only way to *Brahmānanda*.

https://youtu.be/L0PV8ukCHH

Mahāvākya Vichāra - Aham Brahma Asmi

Speaker: Shri Jaishankar Narayanan

There are not only four *mahāvākyas* but there are many more in the *Upaniṣads*. Each *mahāvākya* is an identity equation, which equates two apparently different things as identical. The protagonists of duality claim that *jīva* may have some qualities like *Īśvara* but it can never be equated to *Īśvara*. Because, one is limited and the other is limitless. Advaita does not disagree with that part of the disclaimer which says: as far as *pratyakṣa* (transactional world) is concerned there is certainly a difference. But equality comes according to *Advaita*, when you look at the *dharmī* instead of the *dharma*. Ocean and waves may be different from an outward perspective. But deeper within, both are only water; that is the look of them as dharmī and not as their *dharma*.

He entered the manifest world, says the *Upaniṣad*. The limitless one cannot enter the limited one. So what is the correct meaning? *Śaṅkara* comes to our help. '*Guhāyām pravishTah'* means he is now available in the cave of the heart. He is now available as a *sākṣī* in your system.

If one is not *Brahman*, and he is said to become *Brahman*, then that attainment is bound by space and time and so cannot last. In reality one who is already *Brahman*, has slipped from that knowledge by sheer ignorance and so removal of that ignorance brings him back to *Brahmanhood*.

Another *pūrvapakṣa* (opponent of *Advaita*) says: *jīva* is *samsāri* and *Brahman* is *asamsāri*; therefore the *mahavākya aham Brahma asmi* is only for '*sampad-upāsana*. Usually this *upāsana* is doing *upāsana* of the *sālagrāma* as *Viṣṇu*. *Sampad upāsana* is superposing one thing on another; it is only for cognition; cognition cannot produce anything. '*Aham Brahma-asmi'* is not for *upāsana*. It is a statement of fact. A dream tiger is able to wake you up and after waking there is no dream tiger. So also the teaching of '*aham Brahma asmi'* is a means to wake you up so that you are far above the teaching and the taught; because you are now awake to *Brahman*-hood; you are *Brahman*!

There is another *pūrvapakṣa* according to which*jīva* probably is both *Brahman* and not-*Brahman*. This is absurd. A woman cannot be half-woman and half-old! Then they question: Can you show me the Self? The eye cannot see itself. But you can know whether the eyes can see or not. You (*ātman*) are the seer of sight, hearer of hearing, thinker of thought and knower of knowledge. Knowing the knower is not a subject-object relationship. It is impossible to objectify ourselves. The only method is to make Ignorance go away and '*aham Brahma asmi'* is realised!

https://youtu.be/_AGMRSjvufs

Avasthātraya Prakriyā - The Three States of Being

Speaker: Swami Sarvapriyananda

The Absolute Reality is one's own Self. How to make it a living reality for us? The methodology for this is one of *drik driśya viveka* or *panchakośa-prakriyā*. But the most precious *prakriyā* is that of *Māṇḍūkyopaniṣad* (shortened as Ma.U.) known as *avasthā-traya-prakriyā*. These are the pointing devices to the infinite awareness of the immortal existence of our Self. The *bhakti* methodology which is most common with all theistic religions is usually easily understood. The *yoga* methodology which involves extra-normal experiences through meditation is also there. But *Advaita* is radically different. It says: The Absolute Reality, which is Knowledge itself, which is Infinite Bliss is already with us; we already are that, right here and now! What separates us from that Knowledge is our own

Ignorance. So the *prakriyā* is to know and realise. This *prakriyā* (of Ma.U.) does not wait for any extra-ordinary experience (as in Yoga or *bhakti*), but it is based on our three states of experience: Waking, Dream and Sleep– therefore available to everyone. The most powerful Ma. U. takes us by the hand and leads us. It uses an enquiry into these three states to point us to the Truth. Just as, somebody points us to the rope, by saying, 'What you think is a snake, is actually the rope'. *Vedānta* is not interested in either your content of waking experience or in your dream; it is only interested in the experiencer, the dreamer. With his usual *prasanna-gambhirata* (majestic clarity), *Bhagavatpāda Śaṅkara* begins with the statement of *Māṇḍūkyopaniṣad 'soyam-ātma catuśpādah'*.

There are three kinds of experiences in all of our lives: Waking, Dreaming, Sleeping. The *ātma*is explained in its four aspects, using these three experiences. Through the instruments of knowledge, we experience the gross physical world; the experiencer, namely, ourselves, is called *viṣva*. Next stage is the dream stage: I lose sight and awareness of anything physical about me, including my own body, and the dream appears as true at the time of its appearance (*svakāle satyavat bhāti*). The experience in the dream has a different time and space concept and also a different body. The dreamer then, which is ourselves, is called *taijasa*. In the deep sleep state I have no experience, because the mind, etc. have all gone to sleep; it is all a mass of darkness. Later we say: 'I slept like a log (or 'mud' in Bengali). In this state the Self is called *prajña*. When we come back, the earlier waking state and experience comes back.

Now the *Upaniṣad* comes to its climax in the 7th Mantra. It says there is a fourth aspect (which is not familiar to us) called *caturtham* in the *Upaniṣad* and *Śaṅkara* calls it *turīyam*. It says the fourth is the foundation, substratum, for the other three. The fourth is NOT a state. It is not the sleeper, not the dreamer, not the one awake, it is not something in between, it is not also inert (*jaḍa*), it is not an object for any of the ten senses, and it is not amenable for transactions (*avyavahāryam*). It is invisible (*adriśyam*) and also *alakṣaṇam* (un-inferable). It is unnamed (*avyapadeṣyam*) and also cannot be objectified (*agrāhyam*). It is *ekātma-pratyaya-sāram* – It is the 'I'-cognition. It is (roughly) like the Chief

Station Master standing on the platform watching the busiest trains go by *(jāgrad avasthā)*, the (silent) goods train go by (*svapna avasthā*) and then the blank platform with no activity (*suṣupti avasthā*). It is the One Consciousness watching all the three states. *Prapanchopaṣamam ṣāntam*, the world itself which was only an appearance and even that is quiet now. It is now *shāntam* beyond all suffering or experience. This is the Ultimate which is beyond Time, Space and Causation. The only thing between us (mind, etc.) and this *turīya* is our own stupid Ignorance, which we don't even recognise.

This *turīya* is not just another aspect just as the earlier three are. It cannot be expressed in any way except by statements of negation; because it is beyond *nāma, rūpa,* and *vyavahāra*. Gold ornaments could be of, say, three kinds – necklace, bangle, ring. But gold is the basis for all. They are all made of the same substance. Their real ingredient is the same. Our real ingredient in all our three states is the same one Consciousness that is the *turīya* or *chaturtham*.

Finally, the statement *'Īśvara-gurur-ātmeti'* is embedded even in our reasonably spiritually mature mind that the *Īśvara* or Guru 'up above' has to be identical with our *ātma* in us. It is not the *Īśvara* that is identical with the self, with all its qualities of creation, etc., but the *Īśvara* without the *Īśvaratvam* (all that makes it *Īśvara*) is what is identical with the Self.

The *sandhyā-vandanam* that scriptures speak of can also be interpreted in the context of techniques of meditation as the 'unthinking gap' between two successive thoughts. The gap is the *sandhyā* (separating point) between two thoughts just as the *sandhyā* is the separating point between day and night.

https://youtu.be/KBH1WKJrzJ

Upāsana and its Importance to a Mumukṣu

Speaker: Swami Chidrupananda

Bhagavad Gītā says only after a long number of births one gets on the path of spiritual ascent to the Supreme. For all you know you might have already gone through all those numerous births. So let us not postpone our yearning for the Supreme or Knowledge of Him thinking that it may not happen in this birth and one has a long way to go! Take it that you have come a long way and make efforts right away in this very birth itself. And the only unavoidable means is *upāsana* (Continued absorption in His thoughts, worship of Him and spiritual meditation prescribed in almost every *Upaniṣad*). It is *upāsana* of a form or name of the Absolute that will surely take you on the right track for Ultimate Realisation of the Blissful Supreme as your very Self.

It is mostly the mind (*antaḥkaraṇa*) that has to be wholly involved in this process. It is this instrument of the mind that is always subjected to various distractions by the mundane world. It needs more strength of will-power to protect your aspirations for doing *sādhanas*. Maintain continuity of thought of the Supreme, uninterrupted by dissimilar thoughts by having an object of meditation as something (*devata, kuladevata*, temple-located *vigraha* or *sālagrama* and *bānalinga* in your own *puja,* whatever) which is sanctioned by scriptures. The fifth chapter of *Chāndogyopaniṣad* gives you various alternatives.

You may be doing obligatory duties or rituals for particular ends. Even here to enrich the fruits of such *karmas* you need to resort to *upāsana. Upāsana* is a mano-vritti – i.e. modification of the mind. It will lead you to *Advaita-jñāna* (Realisation of the Self) in the long run. The fact that we are not able to progress in the pursuit of the goal of *Advaita* is because we have, knowingly or unknowingly superimposed all our duality-created differences on our Self. *Upāsana* is the antidote to dissolve this *adhyāsa* (superimposition). Upāsana slowly dissolves your *vāsanas* also. The Vasanas get exterminated, though gradually, like camphor in fire. They don't germinate any further. Though you are already a *mukta* (liberated one) you don't recognize it because you have not yet felt the unreality (*mithyātvam*) of the world around you. *Mithyātvam* is not total unreality like a square-circle or a lotus in the sky or offspring of a barren woman. It is something which appears as existence but has its own end by disappearing.

Upāsana (either *puja* or *japa* or *dhyana*) is sure to expand your mind-visualisation. That is the road to a *vishāla-buddhi*. In summary, *upāsana*achieves three things: purification of the mind; concentration and single-pointedness; and the expansion of one's vision to the cosmic level. And all this will bring the burning desire for *ātma-vicara* in you. The *Kaivalya Upaniṣad* extols the chanting of *Rudra-adhyāya* from the *Veda*, so highly, that, according to it the very vibration of those sounds from the *Rudram* through its mantra-effects can lead you to the very Realisation of the Self.

Bhagavad Gītā also extols in the same way the *upāsanas* through either or many of *nāma, rūpa, guṇa* or *kriyā*. For those who are continually engaged in such *upāsana*, Kṛṣṇa says, the Supreme will give the *buddhi-yoga* (Ch.10) that will take him up on the spiritual ascent.

https://youtu.be/D-uwYkKm28E

Satkāryavada

Speaker: Dr. Ganesh Ishvar Bhat

The whole talk was extremely technical though excellently delivered in Sanskrit. The subject is the analysis of *kāraṇa*(cause) and *kārya* (Effect). The main question is the nature of the relationship between *jagat* and *Brahman*. One is the effect and the other is the cause. In what sense? Did the effect exist in the cause before it appeared as an effect? If that is so it is called '*sat-kārya-vāda*'. If it does not, it is '*asat-kārya-vāda*'. Now philosophers go into rhapsodies on this question. This talk was one such, but most enjoyable (though difficult to follow the logic, because it was in sanskrit).

The effect existed in the cause, already, even before the effect appeared. This is *satkāryavāda*. Maybe this should be called '*sat-kāraṇavāda*'. The *satkāryavāda* is already in *Chāndogya Upaniṣad*.

The cause 'became' the effect. This is *pariNāma vāda.* But this is not supported by *śruti.*

When the effect does not exist in the cause, it is called '*ārambha-vāda'*. One school of philosophy, named *vaiśeṣika,* hold this view.

There is a *sanghāta vāda* by the Buddhists.

The standard examples that go into the discussion are:

Shell appears as silver. Shell only appears; not 'becomes' silver. This is only an optical illusion.

Rope appearing as a snake. Rope in twilight appears as a snake. No becoming

Water appearing in a mirage. Again, only appearance.

Clay and clay-pot. This example creates all the possibilities!

https://youtu.be/8R6EIdC6pi4

Panchakośa Prakriyā

Speaker: Shri Kalyankumar

A *prakriyā* is a *pratikalpanā* or counter fiction as opposed to *svābhāvika kalpanā* which makes us think about God and the universe in our own way. *Brahman* that encompasses and pervades everything is not available for our understanding or realisation because of our Ignorance. Knowledge of *Brahman*, its largeness and unlimited nature is the solution. So the *Vedas* have a *prakriyā* for us by means of an *Upaniṣadic* strategy known as *adhyāropa-apavāda* – i.e., superimposition and sublation. At any level you are a part of the totality (*samaṣṭi*); but you think you are limited. So the *prakriyā* of *panchakośa vichāra* gives you a different way of looking at what you already know. The trick of the *Upaniṣads* to teach you may also be known as *śākhā-candra-nyāya*. The moon on Shukla Tritiya the third day of brighter fortnight (which must be seen, acc. to scriptures) may not be visible easily. So you are shown a nearby tree, and its branches and other extensions, through one of which you are asked to look at the sky and the three-day old crescent is visible in the direction through the branches you are shown. *Śakhā* is a branch of the tree.

In the same way, *Brahman* which is not realisable easily is shown through various stages of things well known to you, namely, Physical food; Activational Energy; Emotional Mind; Intellectual Wisdom and Enjoyable Bliss. This is the way we have to proceed as a *prakriyā* (means of knowing) because we are all otherwise dissatisfied, uneasy and unhappy. We do not know or understand that we are ourselves the *Brahman*; so *Upaniṣad* uses the idea from the tenth man-story. It makes you 'complete the count' by yourself and then when you are stuck it 'completes the count'. In other words it makes you think (this is *adhyāropa*) that the totality of bodies made of food is *Brahman* and then itself (by negating the earlier understanding) takes you to the next stage of cosmic energy (totality of all *prāṇas*). This way it goes on to the next stage of the *samaṣṭi* of the *manas* and then the *samaṣṭi* of the *vijñāna,* intellectual wisdom. This process of slow and steady *vichāra* (enquiry) is what is leisurely described in the *Taittirīyopaniṣad.* At each stage just as the pot is produced by clay and is therefore pervaded by clay, each level – *annam, praṇa, manas, vijnaāna* – is pervaded in full by the next subtler and higher level and finally *vijñāna-maya kośa* itself is pervaded in full by *ānandamayakośa.* In each case you are first concentrating on the lower level (just as you are looking at a branch of a tree rather than the moon which is yonder) and then the *apavāda* (the negation) comes and makes you take the next higher level as *Brahman.* The fifth level is the *ānandamayakośa* and just beyond, the 'count' is completed by the *Upaniṣads*, and you are told *Brahman* is what pervades the totality of *ānanda* and therefore all the earlier ones!

https://youtu.be/uAoSNYSplNI

Brahmasūtra Catuḥssūtrī: An Introduction

Speaker: Prof. K Ramasubramanian

Brahmasūtra is one of the most important texts of *Vedānta* by *Vyasāchārya* and has 555 *sūtra-s* divided into 192 topic-wise sections (*adhikaraṇas*). These sūtras primarily present the rationale for arriving at the import of a few sentences of *Upaniṣads* that are likely to create confusion in terms of their import and which may seem to be in contradiction to each other. The set of first four sūtras of *Brahmasūtra* is widely studied and is popularly known as "*Catuḥssūtrī*". This talk focussed on the content of the first *adhikaraṇa* of *Brahmasūtra*, based on the commentary by *Bhagavatpāda-Śaṅkarāchārya* and the further commentary by *Vācaspatimisra* ("*Bhāmatī*").

The first four sūtras are: *athāto Brahmajijñāsā* (Thereafter, hence, a deliberation on *Brahman*);

janmādyasya yataḥ (That from which the universe had its birth); *śāstrayonitvāt* (omniscient because of being the source of scriptures); *tattu samanvayāt* (But that *Brahman* being the object of full import).

In each *adhikaraṇa*, there are five elements structured into it: they are: *viṣaya* (Subject), *samśaya* (Doubt), *pūrvapakṣa* (Prima Facie opinion). *siddhānta* (Final conclusion) and *sangati* (connection with previous sūtra). In the preface to his *bhāṣya*, *Śaṅkara* devotes one long paragraph called *adhyāsa bhāṣya. Adhyāsa* means cognition of one thing as what it is not.. The first sūtra means: After gaining the four-fold qualification the desire to know *Brahman* leads to enquiry. The four qualifications are discrimination between real and unreal, a dispassion for things either of this world or of the higher worlds, the endowment of qualities śama, dama etc. and an irrevocable objective to attain *mokṣa*.

Then the reverential inquiry (*mīmāṃsā*) of the sentences of *Vedānta* which convey the oneness of the individual self and *Brahman* (*jīva-Brahmaikya*) starts. The import (*tātparya*) of

Vedānta is that the primordial entity (*Brahman*) and the true nature of the innermost self (*ātman*) are one and the same. It is our ignorance (*avidyā*) taking the form of superimposition (*adhyāsa*) that prevents us from realizing this oneness, which is the cause of all kinds of problems (*anartha-hetu*). To explain this dispassion and removal of *adhyāsa*, it is easy to recall our common experience wherein something happens to 'not you' (say to spouse, to offspring, or to property or to your body) and you supposed and felt it as having happened to you! *Vedānta* calls it '*bāhya dharma*s' and are superimposed as '*ātma-dharma*s'.

Vedānta further ascertains that the self-knowledge (*ātma-vidyā*) alone, by eradicating this ignorance, leads to the ultimate freedom (*mokṣa*). Is it ever possible to do this sort of inquiry in any meaningful way? The Prima facie view is no, because it does not always bring about *mokṣa*. There is no cause-effect relationship between the inquiry and *mokṣa*.

The *siddhāṃta* is established: It is possible. The self-knowledge takes place, once the four-fold qualification (*sādhana-catuṣṭaya*) – discrimination (*viveka*), detachment (*virāga*), six-fold wealth (*sampat*), and desire for freedom (*mumukṣutva*) – is cultivated by the student.

In this context, *Vācaspatimisra,* the author of *Bhāmati* introduces an interesting discussion, which is worth reading in the original. He presents an objection that it seems to be impossible to have *virāga*, because everyone has attachment towards pleasure, and aversion towards pain. For example, one does not mind going through the pain of removing thorny scales, to experience the pleasure of eating fish. It is not that people do not engage in activities like sowing seeds, simply because there are possible troubles, such as wild animals which may eat crops. In response, he points out that self-knowledge is the ultimate human pursuit (*parama-puruṣārtha*), and concludes that *Brahman* should be inquired after gaining the four-fold qualification. But *Brahman* cannot be known from any other source because the scriptures are the only valid means of knowledge. *Brahman* is the object of the fullest import of all the *Upaniṣads*.

https://youtu.be/Nk9L-ARAR20

Brahmasūtra's Anandamayadhikaraṇam: a Critical Study

Speaker: Dr. Gauri Mahulikar

This talk is on the seminal argument of originality and logic by the colossal intellect that was *Śaṅkara's*. The subject is the *'ānandamaya'*, the fifth such mentioned in *taittitīya Upaniṣad*. The other four, *'annamaya'*, *'prāṇamaya'*, *'manomaya'*, *'vijñānamaya'* are not the Absolute *Brahman* - this conclusion is understood by everybody, because there is still a fifth mentioned as subtle-most (you may call it 'innermost' – if you want to compromise with accuracy). The fifth is *'ānandamaya-kośa'*. Now the problem is: Is *'ānandamaya'* the ultimate Absolute *Brahman* or not? This is the topic of this whole talk based on Śaṅkara bhāṣya of the arguments in I-i-12 to 19 of Brahmasūtra. The excellence of the advocacy qualities of *Śaṅkara* comes specially from the fact that he puts himself in his opponent's side of logic, presents it as the opponent's argument and then smashes it himself by giving logical counter-arguments. This happens two times in sūtras 12 to 19. Typically it goes like this wherein I have probably over-simplified it:

Some technical symbolism: '*Purva-pakṣa*' means an opponent's view (Usually this is *Śaṅkara's* own coined opposition; Also this may not always be the same opponent. *Śaṅkara* puts himself in the views of various opponents). '*Vedānta-pakṣa*' means *Śaṅkara's* rejoinder to and refutation of the *pūrva-pakṣa* views. *Śaṅkara* finally establishes in the finale that *ānanda* is *Brahman*, not *ānandamaya*. This kind of repeated extra logic and as-if-irrefutable arguments for the statements he makes is a marathon skill of dialectics, that are peculiarly *Śaṅkara's*. Dr. Gauri presents it beautifully because of her own thorough understanding of the *bhāṣya*. Here given only a bare outline of the subject in a very condensed manner. It will be better for readers of this synopsis (if they want to get a full taste of it) to go back to the actual talk of Dr. Gauri.

Also '*ānanda-maya*' is translated (following Swami Gambhirānanda) in English as 'The Blissful'. *Śaṅkara* has a prologue to this discussion. He reminds us of two facets of *Brahman*, namely '*sopādhika*' (with attributes) and '*nirupādhika*' (without attributes). The first one is for *upāsana* and the second one is to be known (as Knowledge).

Pūrvapakṣa 1: '*Ānandamaya* cannot be *Brahman*' because he is included in the series of secondary selves, *annamaya*, *praṇamaya*, etc.

Śaṅkara: But he is the innermost of all

Pūrvapakṣa 1: He is said to possess limbs, etc. acc. to Upaniṣad

Śaṅkara: Only in reference to the Supreme Self, the word bliss is repeated. (And *Śaṅkara* quotes a no. of sentences from *Taittirīyopaniṣad*, ch.2, *Anuvāka* 7 and 8).

Pūrvapakṣa1: The suffix '*maya*' denotes 'modification' and so it is not the Absolute.

Śaṅkara: The suffix *maya* is used in the sense of 'abundance'. One who delights others (acc. to U.) must be possessed of an abundance of bliss. Also the sequence of various 'not-self's' *annamaya* etc. is something like the *Arundhatinyāya*, where the real Arundhati star happens to be the one mentioned last after the indication of many stars, which are assumed to be Arundhati. Having come to this stage, Śaṅkara takes this conclusion as that of pūrvapakṣa 2 and starts refuting it

Pūrvapakṣa2: Thus we see that *ānandamaya* is *Brahman.*

Śaṅkara. Then by the same argument you will have to conclude that the other four, namely *annamaya*, *prāṇamaya*, etc., should also be *Brahman*!

Pūrvapakṣa 2: *Brahman* is an independent entity. Why is it then presented as a limb of the Blissful one in the text: *Brahma pucchham pratiṣṭhā*?

Śaṅkara: It is only to say that the *Brahman* supports the 'blissful one'. *Pucchha* (tail) indicates that it is the substratum.

Dr. Gauri gives a commonplace analogy for the word '*maya*': 'My daughter-in-law' is like my daughter'. This does not mean that they are the same. The word 'like' has an emphasis of its own.

So also *ānandamaya* cannot be taken as *ānanda* itself.

The text of the *bhāṣya* of *Brahmasūtra* is much more detailed, specific, and nerve-racking in its logic than this simple extract.

https://youtu.be/DIPnqwkRG9g

Adhyāsa Bhashya- A Jewel by Śaṅkara

Speaker: Swamini Svatmavidyananda

The digest of this talk is going to be very meagre, because the topic is a top one (as BITS students used to say: 'OHT'=Over the head Transmission!). *Adhyāsa bhāṣya* is just an introductory (small) chapter to the massive *Brahmasūtra bhāṣya* of *Bhagavatpāda Śaṅkarāchārya*. The introduction is also by him. The style of this brilliantly worded introduction is known to have a unique '*prasannatā*' (= exciting and comforting nature) and '*gambhIratā* (= seriousness, profundity and majesty). The 555 aphorisms of *Brahmasūtra* are supposed to be studied only after you have assimilated *Upaniṣads* and *Bhagavad Gītā*, not for one-upmanship but to get perfect clarity in *Vedānta* and this introduction doubles up as both an introduction to the Sutras as well as the entire Vedānta knowledge. The content of this introduction is so compactly packed but it still eradicates the layer of Ignorance in us. The very first words are torrential: (*yuṣmad asmat pratyaya gocarayoh viṣaya viṣayiṇoh tamaḥprakāśavadviruddhasvabhāvayoh*)

The 'you'-cognition (*yuṣmat-pratyayaH*) is the cognition (*pratyaya*) of an object as 'this'.

The 'I'-cognition is the subject (cognified as such by the subject itself).

This object-subject relationship is a relationship of contrariety just like 'darkness' and 'light'.

The *jagat-Brahma* cognition is also similar.

The cognizer and the cognized is like the person and his shadow. If the shadow falls on water the cognizer is not affected by the cold of the water. So what happens to the shadow should be of no concern to the cognizer.

The 'I'-cognition is Knowledge itself. When I see the flower we say, 'I know the flower'. Flower is only a manifestation of whatever is 'this'. Flower is not self-evident, it does not advertise its presence as 'I am the flower'. It is *anātma*.

The objects of cognition and the cognizer should not therefore be mixed. Any such mix-up (like darkness versus Light) is nothing but Ignorance.

The world, which appears, is to be used as a pole, like a pole-vaulter uses the pole to cross over to the other side and leaves the pole. We cross over to *Brahman* using what appears as *jagat (*universe). In other words the duality of *jagat* and *Brahman* is used as a medium to cross over to the non-duality of the omnipresent *Brahman*.

The fact that 'I' is non-negatable is what is meant by '*svatah-siddham'* (self-evident) All the things that 'I' cognises can neither be described as 'existing' nor described as 'non-existing'. They are called *mithyā*. That is why *Jagat* is *mithyā* and *Brahman* is the Eternal Truth.

In fact there is also a mutual superimposition. In the 'I' almost often 'not I' is projected as when we say 'I am blind' 'I am fat' 'I am angry'.

The *adhyāsa* or superimposition is thus the mix-up of *mithyā* with the Absolute Existence that is *Brahman*.

https://youtu.be/ASx-fD1BTHs

Drk Driśya Viveka

Speaker: Swamini Brahmaprakashananda Saraswati

Drik is Seer. *Driśya* is whatever is seen. There is a fundamental distinction between the two. The analysis of this distinction is *drik-driśya-viveka* which is a *prakaraṇa grantha*, usually ascribed to *Ādi Śaṅkarāchārya* himself. A *prakaraṇa grantha* is a later exposition of some aspects of the earlier *śruti* and the *Upaniṣads*. Tattvabodha, Vivekachudamani, *Vedānta sāra* – are all such *prakaraṇa* granthas; each one starts from a certain context and independently explains as much of the whole *Vedānta śāstra* as possible, as a sort of teaching. *Drik Driśya Viveka* starts from the fundamental problem of the difference between the seer and the seen and how it is that the ordinary people fail to realise it. The world is *driśya*m (the seen, not the seer); My body also is *driśyam*, not the seer. What about the eyes? In a preliminary sense the eye is the seer. But not really. For, a *driśya*m (object) undergoes change – world, body, my hand, fingers, all undergo change. What about the eyes? They also undergo change, because there are eyes which are sharp, eyes which have dull vision, and eyes which are blind. So eyes also are *driśyam*. But who is the seer of the eyes? The mind is the seer of the eyes. But is mind changeless? No. Mind also changes, because there are various stages (*vrittis*) of the mind. So mind cannot be the seer always. Who sees the mind? The Consciousness within (*śudda-caitanyam*) sees the mind, which has changes like *kāma, sankalpa*, shame (*hrIh*), doubt, belief, etc. Now consciousness never changes. So consciousness is the final *drik*. Everything else is a *driśya*m. This Consciousness is also called *kūṭastha, pratyagātma* (Inner Self), *caitanyam*, etc. This consciousness never becomes an external *driśyam*. It has nothing of the well-known six-fold changes, namely, birth, existence, growth, modifications, decline and destruction. Consciousness is *svayam-prakāsha* – without any *sādhana* it shines. On the other hand, everything which is *driśya* needs a *sādhana* for it to see something; like the eyes which always need light to see.

Now there is a question. If the final *drik*, namely, consciousness or *ātma* has no change, but everything else which is seen, undergoes changes, for whom is the *mokṣa* stage prescribed? If I am the unlimited Consciousness why do I feel I am limited? This is where the idea of reflected consciousness *(jīva)* in the *buddhi* comes. (*cidābhāsa* or *chit-chāyā*). By the entry of consciousness in the *buddh*i, sentience occurs for the mind, which has two facets: *kartritva* and *kāraṇa*. The *kāraṇa* facet of the mind is the so-called *antaḥkaraṇa*. The *kartritva* facet of the *buddhi* or mind is the so-called functional ego (*ahamkara*, not the villain-type ego of ordinary understanding, but simply the 'I am'-ness). This 'I am'-ness shines and glows like a red hot iron ball, where we cannot distinguish between the ball and the fire. So also we cannot distinguish the consciousness (which is the 'light' of the fire) from the *buddhi* and *buddhi*-mind thinks it is itself sentient consciousness. And this sentience gets transferred (as a pervasion) to all the parts of the body. So this borrowed 'sentience' of the *buddhi* pervades the entire parts of the body just as a *marakata* (jade) gem immersed in milk makes the entire milk blue or coloured. Just as we cannot distinguish between the fire and the iron ball, so also we cannot distinguish between the BMI and the borrowed consciousness (sentience) which has pervaded it. It is only *Vedāntic* knowledge obtained from a teacher that can rectify this innate mistake or ignorance in us. In short there are only five things: existence, knowledge (that shines) and bliss – these three are eternal; and two more, namely name and form which are ephemeral.

https://youtu.be/BZMvFRQLRwA

Kārya Kāraṇa Vāda

Speaker: Swami Tattvavidananda Saraswati

'The *kāraṇa* (Cause) for the universe is Brahman'. This is a general understanding of most of us from the *Upaniṣads*. But *Brahman* being *nirguṇa,* cannot be a *kāraṇa.* So let us go to the rope-snake analogy. Is the rope the cause for the snake? No. Rope did not do anything, did not transform itself as a *pariṇāma* (transformation or change) to become the snake, did not manifest itself to show itself as a snake. It is all because of the ignorance of our mind that the snake 'appears'. So also, the universe only 'appears' because of our ignorance. When we say *Brahman* is the 'Cause' (*kāraṇa*) for the universe, we are only attributing (*kalpanā)* to *Brahman* the 'state of a cause' (*kāraṇatvam*); this should be the meaning of the *Upaniṣadic* statement "*tadātmānam svayam akuruta*" – meaning, it, the *Brahman* by itself appears as universe, not transformed. Just as the apprehension of a snake (in the rope-snake analogy) is a mistake or error, so also our understanding of the appearing universe as real is a mistake. Correct it and you are done. Because Śaṅkara repeatedly uses the phrase '*tad-ananyatvāt*' to say that the universe is not different from *Brahman*, because there is nothing else other than *Brahman*. The phrase '*anya*' means different or other. The phrase '*ananya*' means 'not other', 'not different'. And '*vyatirekeṇa abhāvah*' is another characteristic expression of Śaṅkara. It means, 'non-existence as a different entity'. You cannot say that from the transcendental point of view there is rope, and from the operational point of view there is snake. What appears as a snake is non-different from the rope. *Jagat* or Universe therefore is not 'other' than *Brahman*. It is *Brahman*! The whole *Vedānta* is to tell us that we have to dismiss the appearance. Even Science tells us to dismiss the idea that 'sun rises in the east and sets in the west' if you want to know the truth. So the '*neti, neti*' formula of the *Upaniṣad* is gives the '*vivarta vāda*' of Advaita its essence in the form of *kāraṇa-kārya-vaada*.

https://youtu.be/OFmX0dYwVNA

Adhyāsa-Mithyā-Māyā: An Overview

Speaker: Swamini Paraprajnananda

Seeing one thing or another is *adhyāsa.* This is *atat-buddhi* (*atat* means what is not real). This is our major error. How can life be successful if we start with this error? This is the cause of all our miseries. So *Ācārya Śaṅkara* says in his Preamble to *Brahmasūtra bhāṣya*, 'We need to do the enquiry of *Brahman* (*Brahma vichāra*). The śāstra tells you that you are making a colossal error. The *Upaniṣads* declare: You are the *ātman*, Your nature is *ānanda*, happiness. It is necessary to correct our thinking. The 'I' and the 'Object' (*asmat and yuṣmat*) are mutually exclusive. Like Light and Darkness. The 'I' can never be superposed on the *viṣaya*, which is the Object. 'I' is *viṣayī* (the knower) Attributes of *viṣaya* (object, the known) can never be the *dharma*s of 'I'. The attributes of 'Snake' and the attributes of the 'rope' cannot be mixed with each other. Even though this is impossible this has happened in all our lives. This superposition itself is *mithyā*.

Even though this superposition of the unreal on the real is not logical we, because of our colossal beginning-less Ignorance, have made it possible. In other words we have combined *satya* (Truth) with *mithyā* (which exists and also does not exist). *Cit* and *jada* mixing is what has happened. You are the Knower, never the known. This is an unholy wedlock! All our worldly transactions are based on this damage. The limitless *ātman*, (= 'I') is being taken as limited. And we keep saying: I don't want misery or insecurity. Neither misery nor insecurity belongs to us. For instance we say 'I am fat; I am this, I am that…' etc. *Dharma* of sense organs (like fatness, tallness, etc.) and *antaḥkaraṇa (=mind) dharma*s (like I am happy, I am sorrowful, etc.) are all superposed on 'I'. What is needed is to destroy this error, burn our boats and study the *śāstras* to know your true Nature.

The saving grace is that this *adhyāsa* is not absolutely real. The fact that what is happening is *mithyā* is the saving grace. The Universe (*jagat)* as well as the status of a *jīva* (*jīvatvam*) are both *mithyā*. The *nirvikāra* (changeless) *Brahman* is the Absolute Reality. *Mithyā* cannot be said to have either absolute existence or absolute existence or both. No categorical statement can be made. That is the definition of *mithyā*; because it has no substantiality.

In *Chāndogya Upaniṣad Uddālaka* says to Svetaketu: By knowing the One Absolute Truth you know everything. All changes that appear are only verbal (*vācārambhanam*). Name and form of clay pot are only words. If we remove the clay there is no pot. So the pot is not separate from clay. Pot is only appearance. Thus what we call creation, *jīva, jagat* is all *mithyā*. *Brahman* undergoes no change. 'Clay is the Truth' (*mrittiketyeva satyam*). *Bhagavad Gītā* (B.G.) śloka '*nāsato vidyate bhāvo....*'says exactly this. Neither *shoka* (sorrow) nor *moha* (delusion) nor change (*vikāra*) is there. They all only appear; so they are *mithyā*. *Mithyā* cannot stand on its own. The snake that appears on the rope, has no appearance of its own, without the substratum of the rope. Similarly '*jīvatva*' (status of *jīva*) is *mithyā* on the satya of *Brahman*. jīva and *Brahman* are the same.

Māndūkya kārika declares: What is not present in the beginning and in the end, does not exist in the middle also. (*ādāvante ca yannāsti ....*) In the dream one is the father of a child. But after the dream neither the father is there nor the child.

*Māya*is explained elaborately in Vivekacūḍāmaṇi. The purport of all this *prakaraṇa grantha* is for us to learn *Vedānta* from someone who knows it entirely. Otherwise we may get lost in the forest (*araṇya*) of words. *Māya*does not manifest to you; but its effects are manifest. *Māya* is the *Śakti* (*prakṛti*, nature) and the one who controls is the *māyavī* (the Supreme). It is *māya* that gives the designation of *Īśvara* to the Absolute nameless and formless *Brahman*. *Māya* itself can neither be said to exist or not exist. Therefore it is called *'anirvacanīyam'* (not expressible through words). But *māya* is not independent. It has a substratum, namely *Brahman*. B.G. says '*mayādhyakshena*. Just because of my presence it works, says the Lord. Though *māya* can do almost impossible things possible, you have to overcome *māya* by resorting to the feet of the Lord. Just as, the fish that crawls to the feet of the fisherman does not fall into his net of *māya*!

https://youtu.be/i_V73ivCD58

Adhyāropa-Apavāda Prakriyā: A key to Vedānta

Speaker: Shri V Subramanian

Bhagavatpāda Śaṅkarāchārya cites this maxim in this form in the Bh. *gītā* 13.13 commentary. The *gītā* verse 13.13 is about the availability of *Brahman* for all of us to experience in the living beings that are all endowed with hands, feet, eyes, ears, etc. This is the *adhyāropa*. But this is not to convey that *Brahman* is indeed endowed with these. Hence the *apavāda*, negation of those superimposed earlier, is necessary and that is done in the next verse, 13.14. By doing the *adhyāropa-apavaāda* technique we are able to understand the *Brahman* as the only Truth and the Universe as *mithyā*. This is in Gauḍapādācārya's Uttara *Gītā bhāṣya*. The maxim translates to: 'Deliberate superimposition and subsequent negation.'

We can give some commonly understandable analogies to this maxim: Our worship of the

*Gaṇeśa*idol, where we infuse the divinity into it by *prāna pratishṭhā*, etc., and later remove it by *visarjana*.

Here is an interesting story: A king had 17 elephants. Then the king died. He had three sons. According to his will, the first son was entitled to one-half of the number of elephants, the second to one-third, and the third to one-ninth. The size of the share couldn't be changed. As 17 is an odd number, and difficult to share among the three, they were unable to find a solution to the challenge. Fortunately for them, a wise man was passing through their country. He was an old friend of their father's as well. The young men described their predicament and asked for his help. The wise man asked them not to worry and set about solving the problem immediately.

He added his own elephant to the 17 elephants; they were now 18. He separated 9 elephants or one-half of 18, and gave them to the first son. The second son was given six elephants or one-third of 18. Lastly, the third son was given two elephants, two being one ninth of 18. The total number of elephants given away was 17 (9+6+2). The eighteenth elephant left was that of the wise man who took his elephant back and left, with everybody happy and satisfied. The last elephant is like *māya*: it came to solve a problem, and having solved it, it removes itself from the scene, leaving no trace of its previous presence.

This is the purpose/method of the *adhyāropa – apavāda* in *Vedānta*.

The *'śākhā-candra darshana'* (identifying the crescent moon with the help of a supposed connection with the branch of a tree) and *'sthūla arundhati darshana'* (identifying the Arundhati star by its proximate surrounding celestial objects) maxims are also about this *adhyāropa-apavāda* alone.

There is an unmistakable *adhyāropa-apavāda nyāya* explained in *Māṇḍūkya Upaniṣad*. The Supreme Truth is presented as four-parts in the *Māṇḍūkya Upaniṣad*. This is to facilitate the knowledge of the Supreme Truth by first looking at the Truth as consisting of both *parā* and *aparā* aspects. The *aparā* is shown as the three states: waking, dream and deep sleep. These three have a cause-effect relationship among them: the waking and dream duo is the effect and their cause is the deep sleep state. The effect too is further stated as – the waking is gross, the dream as subtle and deep sleep being the causal. *Turīya,* the Ultimate Truth, however, transcends the cause- effect world. *Turīya*, therefore, is Pure, beyond the cause-effect duality.

In the commentary to the 7th mantra in the *Māṇḍūkya* the *adhyāropa – apavāda* is clearly brought out: This *ātman* is four-bodied of which three are non-transcendental and one is transcendental. The three non-transcendental are the ones which correspond to the waking, dream and sleep state. They are like the seed for the plant. Once the plant is understood the seeds are discarded. Actually the seed idea is only an *adhyāropa*. The seedless absolute transcendental one called '*Turīya'* is the only Truth. The three earlier states mentioned are like the *sarpa (*snake) of the rope-snake analogy. So when we discard (*apavāda*) the snake-appearance like three states of waking, dreaming and sleeping, the *Turīya*, the Absolute *Brahman* is known.

https://youtu.be/7eTIiB4AR8M

Śravaṇa, Mananam & Nidhidhyāsanam

Speaker: Swami Tattvarupananda

Everyone wants a type of life-fulfilment, which is beyond the requirements of money, security and limited material time-bound benefits. Ultimate fulfilment cannot be got from the world, where everything is time-bound and space-bound. So what we want is irrespective of time, space and surroundings. First have this *vyavasāyātmikā buddhi* (B.G. (2-41) determined Mind). The problem is we are not in touch with the ānandainside us. This is Self-Ignorance. Self-Knowledge alone can remove this. To know this Reality first keep your body in a healthy state, so that you can forget it. But don't pamper the body. Only respect it and do the bare needful. Because it is the instrument through which you have to learn to get the Ultimate Truth. First get to understand that Action (whether world-oriented or ritualistic which are heaven oriented) will not produce what you are looking for as the Ultimate fulfilment. Means and ends of Karma Kanda of the *Vedas* have limitations. *Jñāna* kanda says through its *Upaniṣads*: Know thyself! You are other than the BMI.

The *sādhana* for this Knowledge (*jñāna*) is through *śravaṇa* (=S), *Manana* (=M) and *Nididhyāsana* (=N).

Now S (=*śravaṇa*) has to be received from one who has learnt the *śāstras* the traditional manner (a *śrotriya*) and one who is already a *Brahma-niśṭhā* (in the sense of the *gītā* or the scriptures). Non-Sampradayik self-advertised teachers would not be able to help you, because they cannot be objective; they will mix their own ideas with *śāstras*. Study under your *śrotriya-guru* for quite a length of time. Follow the *pranipāta* and *pariprashna* of the B.G. (4-34). It is that teacher who will be able to help you to remove the *adhyāropa* of the '*atat*' (= unreal) – that is, the removal of the superimposition of the unreal on the Real. Ignorance can be removed only by S (=*śravaṇa*). 'What I am' is the problem.

But the doubt occurs as to 'What I am'. This doubt can be removed only by 'M' (=*Manana*).

But even the *Upaniṣads*, if you read it without the teacher's help, will confuse you. Reading scriptures without teachers will only increase your doubts. It says 'What the mind thinks is not the reality' ('*yanmanasā na manute...*') at one place and at another place it says 'Reality can be realised only by the Mind' ('*manasaivedam āptavyam.*). The meaning of this apparent contradiction and a large number of similar ones can be cleared only by the process of 'S' from the traditionalised teacher and a consequent 'M' by you. 'S' from the *Ācārya* and a follow-up of 'M' on the recurring questions 'How can I be *Brahman*' will help purify the mind.

The last stage is 'N' (-*Nididhyāsana*) which is dwelling on the 'I am'-ness. 'N' is different from Mediation. In meditation the object is different from you. It is other than you. In 'N' the object is yourself so that the objectification gradually disappears and the subject alone remains.

https://youtu.be/_UelFIoNVc4

Gleanings from Śaṅkara's Sanatsujātīya Bhāṣya

Speaker: Prof. V Krishnamurthy

This is a very minute portion of *Mahābharata* – just 130 ślokas in four chapters. King *Dhritaraṣtra* is worried that the oncoming war might exterminate all his sons. His messenger Sanjaya has come back with a reply from the Pandavas, but he would not divulge it except at the meeting of the royal assembly the next morning. So the King asks his brother *Vidura* to give him company for the night and tell him something good. *Vidura* gives an exposition of various rules of *dharma* and this portion of eight chapters of the *Mahābharata* is studied and treasured as *Vidura Nīti*. At the end of it Vidura says all this is only for use in the material world but it may not lead you to the higher spiritual goal of *amritatvam* (Immortality). This word tastes like honey to *Dhritaraṣtra* who thinks it is Immortality that might save his sons from a catastrophe in the ensuing war. Tell me *Vidura*, he says, about *amritatvam*. But Vidura excuses himself because of his birth from a *Śūdrayoni*, but still, uses his yogic powers to bring *Sanatsujāta* from the higher worlds and requests him to talk about *amritatvam* to the King. For a whole night the all-knowing Sage *Sanatsujāta* spends time with this King and answers his impatient volley of questions. This is I.

Śaṅkarāchārya picks up for his *bhāṣyas* only three things from the *Mahābharata*. The first of them is *Viṣṇu Sahasranāma*, which is narrated by the *sātvic Bhīṣma* to the *sātvic* Yudhishtira. The second is the *Gītōpadēśa* from the *Sātvic* Kṛṣṇa to *Arjuna* who is overcome by a *rājasic* compassion. And the third is this *Sanatsujātīyam*, where the recipient of the teaching is a tamas dominated *Dhritaraṣtra*. And *Śaṅkara* gives so much importance to the contents of *Sanatsujātīyam* that his bhāṣya of it is half as big as that of the *gītā* though the text itself is only one fifth of the *gītā*.

The Sage's answer to the very first question of *Dhritaraṣtra* on '*amritatvam*' comes with a bang. We shall blend *Sanatsujāta's* answers with the bhāṣya of *Śaṅkara* on them. *Sanatsujāta* says it is *pramāda* that is death and the opposite of it, namely, *apramāda* is immortality. The bhāṣya says *pramāda* is a slipping from the eternal natural blissful state of the Self and so not ever slipping from that is Immortality. Another question of the King is 'Who is it that directs us from within?'. *Sanatsujāta* takes this question very seriously and objects to the question itself. For *Śaṅkara* comments that the *Taittirīyopaniṣad* has categorically declared in its 2nd chapter (Anuvaka 7) that anyone who makes even an iota of a difference *(u-daram antaram*) between *Brahman* and the *jīva* has to live in this world with fear. No hope for such a person to get out of this *samsāra*. The next question from the King is simple. Does *dhārmic* work compensate for *adharma*? The answer is a definite 'No' from the Sage. Particularly in the modern context we should understand that any *dhārmic* work has its own good results, and similarly all *adharmic* deeds and thoughts have to be exhausted only by experiencing their punishments. No accounting-like cancellation between *dharma* and *adharma*.

Now *Sanatsujāta* himself introduces a monumental concept that any one who misinterprets the nature of the *ātman* is himself a great sinner. He is called an *ātmāpahāri*, The *dharma* of the ātma is incorrectly spoken as if it is the *dharma* of the BMI and vice versa. A reference to the happiness of sleep as if it is the happiness of the BMI and similarly the use of 'I' in saying I have a body pain have both to be properly analysed in the style of Ramana Maharshi. One has to absorb the elaborate *Śaṅkara bhāṣya* on this to get the proper meanings.

A final question about the *Vedas*. One is 'Do the *Vedas* remove our sins?' The answer is No. And the supplemental question is: If so what is the kind of knowledge that the *Vedas* are supposed to be giving and why is there so much importance given to the *Vedas*? The answer is rather detailed. The essence is that the *Vedas* are only pointers to the Supreme, without them we will never have a way to look for the Supreme in the right direction. But as far as knowledge is concerned, we do not get it by reading the *Vedas* because Knowledge is not something made up of words, it has to arise in the proper mental soil, we only get it through a Guru who has the experience of the Absolute, by having traversed the path that the *Vedas* have charted out.

In fact *Sanatsujāta* comes down from his highest pedestal of knowledge and catalogues for the King, twelve defects of mankind, seven pitfalls of the human mind, twelve positive virtues to be cultivated, and six-fold gateways to Knowledge. Finally he ends up with the observation that one should always be one with the Truth and *Śaṅkara* waxes eloquent in his *bhāṣya* on this.

https://youtu.be/s-Fm21BB-Hw

Śruti vs Anubhava Pramāṇa in Advaita

Speaker: Swami Shudhabodhananda

The original title given to this talk was *śruti* versus *Anubhava pramāṇa*. That makes the two – *śruti* and *anubhava* – as opposite contenders for the *pramāṇa*. *Pramāṇa* means *jñāna-sādhanam*. *Pramāṇa* does not mean proof or authority in *Vedānta*. In *Vedānta,* it is something which is not refutable. It is directly connected to knowledge or *ātmajñāna*.

Atmajñāna is experiential. It is a 24x7 experience. There is no time when *chaitanya* is not there. An experience occurs only when there are all the three members of the *tripuṭi* – namely, the experiencer, the experience and the experienced. In the case of the presence of *caitanya* all three are there; but the problem is we don't recognize it. We are not aware of it. It is the awareness that shows it to you as an experience.

Vedānta makes you enquire into the questions: What you are and what you are not. You need not do anything to know what you are. But you have to do everything to undo your understanding of what you are not. Hunting always after *sukha* (happiness) and removal of unhappiness (*duḥkha-nivarti*) should stop. Your real nature is *mokṣamokṣa.* In *Brahmasūtra bhāṣya Śaṅkara* says: *niratiśaya-ānandarūpah ātmā eva ātmani avasthānam* – i.e. The *ātman* which is already a wonderful incomparable Happiness realised as the Self – is *mokṣa.* Just be as you really are; that is *mokṣa*. It is *Vedānta* that enables you to make a surgery (intrinsic mental self-surgery) in the *anātma* that you are thinking you are, to think of it as the *ātma* that you are.

Mind's very nature is to reflect the *chit* and be a *cidābhāsa*. In ordinary perceptions of the world, what happens is this reflection also reflects the object as an object. That reflection is a *vritti* of the mind. That is what removes the ignorance of the object. The same happens in the knowledge of *Brahman*, except at the final stage. This final stage is where the reflection in the mind has itself assumed the nature of ātman itself. That is the *akhandākara-vritti.* In the *Kaṭhopaniśad śloka–yadā panchāvatiśtanṭe*–it is said that when all the senses are inward with no action and mind also does not function, therein you can realise your own real *svarūpa*.

A simple example. Have three different coloured glass bottles (say red, blue and green) and also a fourth one which is a plain uncoloured glass bottle. Fill up the first one with plain water. The water now appears red. This is the waking stage where our mind is full of what we see and experience. Transfer the same water from the red bottle to the blue bottle. You are now in the dream stage, where you are not conscious of outside experience (as red water) nor of your own existence (as simple uncoloured water). Transfer the same water to the third bottle with green colour. Now the water has lost its all earlier experience. And the plain water bottle represents the *turīya*, in its own natural state.

https://youtu.be/0MBYWY4LpZU

Advaita Bhakti: Shri Śaṅkara and Madhusūdana Saraswati

Speaker: Swami Tattwamayananda

Advaita is more than a concept. It is an experience. Two realities are there: namely the Absolute Reality and the Transactional Reality. The latter is not absolutely real. It only appears as real. This is called the state of *mithyā* (What appears and also disappears). This *mithyā* principle is what bothered the dualistic philosophers and for a whole six centuries they kept on writing so many dialectical works on Indian philosophy, calling the *Advaita* as a *māya* philosophy and thus misunderstanding the central theme of Advaita. The result of this long period of dialectical warfare between advaitic scholars and dualist philosophers was the charge that Advaita did not care for *bhakti*. And this, in spite of the fact that Śaṅkara and all the advaitins who followed him were known to have been doing the five-*devatā* puja and other worships as a daily routine. All the *Śaṅkara mathas* established by him have very elaborate codified procedures for the daily puja in the mutt, which has come down as an unbroken heritage over several centuries. In fact Śaṅkara himself is the author of more than four score unique stotra hymns, unbeatable both in its Sanskrit poetic diction as well as in its devotional content, in both styles, simple as well as sophisticated. Śaṅkara is known to have codified and resurrected the six divisions of worship, called the Shanmata: *Āditya, Ambika, Viṣṇu, Gaṇeśa, Śiva* and *Subrahmaṇya.*

In *Śaṅkara's Śivānandalahari* there is a *śloka* (No 61) (the whole work is a litany of devotion) beginning with: *ankolam nija bija santatih...* It is a classic definition of *bhakti.* It gives you five levels of *bhakti* through five analogies. The seeds of the *aṅkola* tree when they mature on the ground they themselves travel to the base of the tree and join the roots by their own nature. Devotion to God should be like this one-pointed purpose of the *aṅkola* seeds. The second analogy is that of iron filings that are drawn to a magnet. The remaining three are: a chaste wife devoted to the husband, a creeper and the tree around which it winds itself and finally a river which invariably flows toward the ocean and merges with it. *Bhakti*, according to Śaṅkara is the attitude of mind which draws you towards the lotus feet of the Lord in the manner of any one of these five analogies. Of course the last mentioned analogy is the most ideal *bhakti*. In Śaṅkara's *Saundaryalaharī* there are numerous *śloka*s depicting the most moving devotion that can be imagined in any tradition. '*bhavāni tvam dase*' (no 22) is one example.

Madusudana Saraswati of the 15th and 16th centuries wrote a monumental work called *Advaita-Siddhi* and many other works. These works once for all silenced the criticisms and false charges against *Advaita-bhakti*, which had been tarnished by the dialectical discussions that had been prevalent before his time. Both *Madhusūdana Saraswati* and Śaṅkara have by their voluminous contributions established that the highest *vijñāna* (Knowledge of *ātman*) comes only from an overflow of the supreme level of *bhakti* and that too by God's Grace. Such a high level of *bhakti* looks at the whole universe as one family. This is the synchronisation of *bhakti* and Oneness called *Advaita bhakti.*

https://youtu.be/zyiNGIXoE7c

अद्वैत सिद्धान्ते जीवस्य गतिः – The Trajectory of Jīva as per Advaita Siddhānta

Speaker: Shri Kuppa Bilwesha Sharma

If you believe in '*jīvo Brahma eva nāparah*' and are interested in realisation of that *Brahman* in you, then this subject may not interest you. But for all others, this description of *jīva's* journey may educate you to think over your habits and behaviour. We do not see the *jīva* leaving the body, we only see the departure of the *prāna* (by putting a finger at the tip of the nose to check for the breath). But *prāna* leaving the body is only an indication for the *jīva* leaving the body. When the *jīva* goes, the *linga śarira*, comprised of the senses and pranas (all together counted as three), mental storage of *vāsanas*, + *avidya* + Desire + *karma* + an abstraction of mind without the memory - all these together called the eightfold city (*puryashṭakam*) goes along with the *jīva*. By which path? There are two paths: *Dhumādi mārga* (also called *Dakśināyana mārga*) and *Archirādi mārga* (also called *Uttarāyana mārga*).

The karma that goes along depends upon three kinds of karma done during life. The three kinds are: *ishta, pūrta and datta.*

The first one is the ritualistic part of the *Vedas* in the form of the various *yajñas* described in the *Vedas*. The second one is the *laukika* part of the works carried out in the form of *lokānugraha*, like construction of temples, hospitals and charitable houses, digging wells and tanks etc. The third is the giving up of one's own possessions in a dh*a*rmic way.

Dhuma mārga takes the *jīva* to *pitr-loka* also called *candraloka*. Another version of it is also called *svarga lok*a or *devaloka* where you may get all your desires.

The *archirādi mārga* is for those who have been exemplary devotees, done a lot of *upāsanas*, for the purpose of purification of mind.

For those who do not fall into either of the above two categories they go on the path to naraka or another human or animal body.

The so-called *mokṣa* (called by Advaita as Self-Realisation as *Brahman*) can be obtained only in *bhūloka* or *satyaloka* (the world of Creator *Brahmā* = *Hiraṇyagarbha*). So once one has enjoyed the dainties of *svarga* or *pitrlokas*, one has to come back to the *bhū-loka* to continue the path either to *mokṣa* or to the same old paths as before.

When a *jīva* comes back after a stay in another loka, it may come as part of the cloud or rain, get into the grains of the land, get into man's food, then gets into the woman's womb and is born again – if the destination for it is a human body.

The total lesson of all this, is, make haste, as a human, to get into the spiritual path so that you may self-realise either in this or in succeeding *janmas*.

https://youtu.be/iYwIf1cnwIk

Guru-tattva in Śaṅkara's Works

Speaker: Swami Japasiddhananda

Guru is the guiding human force on others that leads to perfection and fulfilment. He destroys Ignorance as per the norms of *dharma.* As *deśika,* he is the one deputed to observe his students and their practices. As *ācārya,* he follows the *śāstras* himself and makes the disciples also follow those teachings. He collects the mind of the disciple and makes it concentrated on one *tattva.* By virtue of his very presence the mind is settled. All this and whatever follows below are extracts from the *bhāṣyas* of *Ādi Śaṅkarācārya* to the various *Upaniṣads*. A living embodiment like the Guru can go very far than just a book. *Padma Purāna* says he is the one who tells you what to do and what not to do.

Śvetashvara Upaniṣad (yo *brahmana*m *vidhadhāti pūrvam...*) says that even the creator *Brahmā* was given the self-knowledge by the Absolute Itself.

The *Yogaśāstra*says his omnipotence is not limited by Time. Shri Ramakrishna says it is the Guru who awakens the spiritual fervour in you.

In his various commentaries, *Ācārya Śaṅkara* says guru is identified with *Brahman* (*brahmātmabhūtah*). Unlike an ordinary teacher, guru is not only endowed with knowledge but has experienced it. He is *śama - damādi - sampannah.*

Why has this to be said of a Guru? Is this not obvious? This has to be said, because, a guru who is a *Brahma-jnāni* may show signs of *jadatva* (inertness) or *unmattatva* (madness), because of his realisation of the Universe as a *mithyā*. So his *śama-dama* etc. qualities have to be emphasized so that the world can recognise his greatness. By the *prakriyās* like *avasthātraya* and *panchakośa,* he shows us the way for Self Realisation.

Finally he is established in the traditional *paramparā;* otherwise we may certainly be misguided by out-of-the-box teachings of so-called independent teachers whose improvisations can lead us to madness. Even in the scientific world nobody starts from zero-knowledge; they rise up only by establishing their findings on the basis of existing knowledge-lineage. Even Narendra, later-to-become Swami Vivekananda, though he was very critical of spiritual gurus (including Shri Ramakrishna himself), after he became the foremost disciple of the Sage, himself emphasizes the importance of an unbroken *paramparā* chain. The Guru himself is the *plava* or *nauka* for us to navigate through the ocean of *sāmsara*. *Samsāra* which is an unending cycle is also like the vast ocean where the waves never end; that is why it is called the ocean of samsara (*bhava-sāgara*).

Why is the Guru needed? Not only does he save our time and energy, but he bequeathed the heritage and bestows authority. He mentors, guides and inspires so long as one is in his vicinity as a *śishya*. The biological father gives only the material body; but the Guru gives the *Brahma-sharīra*. Though *Arjuna* originally talks sermonising himself to *Kṛṣṇa* (in Ch.1 of the *Gītā*), the Lord in the final chapter chides him strongly and categorically tells him to follow the teachings, or else, perish! Such strong injunctions can come only from the Guru. We can never pay off our debt either to our mother or the Guru.

How to find a Guru? If you are as sincere and one-pointed as a lover who runs after his love (this is Sri Ramakrishna's analogy!) you will certainly be taken to him by the Almighty. And once you get him, practise an intense service to him (B.G. 4-34), not caring for any of your own comforts; that will bless you with his Grace and a consequent Realisation of the Supreme.

https://youtu.be/3hM0C6njk

Śaṅkara's Teachings on Jīvanmukti

Speaker: Babaji Bob Kindler

Shri Babaji has to his credit innumerable chart-presentations on every aspect of *Vedānta*. So we just copy down below his presentations on *jīvanmukti* and *jīvanmukta* below in the same order in which they were presented in the talk:

First, on *māya*. It is eternal, illusory, insentient, transforms and changes, is the seed of creation, it is the cause of manifestation, has no beginning or end, there are evolutions similar to it, supports karma and can be recognised as such.

The Status and characteristics of a *jīvanmukta* can be listed as follows:

Enjoys the burgeoning of endless merits;

Ever poised in the *Self-Brahman*;

Experiences freedom ever in this world and body;

Has mastered *karma* and desire;

Is peaceful and impervious to *samsāra*;

Retains no sense of 'I', 'Me' and 'Mine';

Is free of the past, present and future.

He sees sameness everywhere and in everything;

Remains unchanged in pleasure & pain;

His heart is filled with Bliss;

Lives in the body only as a witness;

No identification with the body;

Sees no difference between *Brahman* and Mind;

Remains the same at all times;

Into whom enjoyments enter like rivers entering ocean;

Who is conscious of the dependent reality of the world;

Sees indivisible oneness at all times;

Is free from all the effects of worldliness;

Is free from caste laws, blood ties and name and form;

Sees *Brahman* both in the Sentient and the Insentient

Ceases to follow the dogmas of the world;

Seeing Reality, he has forgotten duality as if it never existed;

Recognises that the soul is pure by its very nature;

And it does not have to be purified by external help.

Regarding *mukti* or *mokṣa*,

It is not a state;

It is not freedom produced or generated;

It is not a result of evolution, development or transformation;

It is not the solving of problems of life;

It is not brought about by some power;

It is not disappearance of weakness;

It is not something to be attained;

It is the eternal condition of the Self

https://youtu.be/TXqdoCxHRwQ

Dhyānasvarūpam: The Nature of Meditation

Speaker: Swamini Vimalananda

The very fact that we say '*dhyān raho*' rather than '*dhyān karo*', shows that Meditation is not an 'action' per se. It is a state of mind to focus itself on an object, in the first instance, and after due practice, focus itself on the Self. But as a starting point, most seekers start focusing on a form of God or on the qualities of God or on the lilas of God. There is a fundamental requirement of alertness of the mind in all techniques of meditation. It may be with eyes open or eyes closed. The oneness of all forms is a sine qua non of meditation of a form. In fact whatever one sees outside can be seen in the mind's eye as a form or quality of God. The Oneness has to be extended even to the extent that you do not separate good from bad, or liking to non-liking. Everything is *satyam* (Truth), *śivam* (Good) and *sundaram* (beautiful). This may be called the massive *Virāṭa* (All-embracing and all pervading) form of the Absolute.

The meditation of various forms is called *saguṇa upāsana*. The *guṇa* itself can be the subject of Meditation also. Whether it is Nature or the vastness and completeness (*pūrṇatvam*) in the Universe, all are proper objects of meditation if they can lead you to a contentment (*tripti*) which is nothing but the reflection of the Absolute in what you meditate on. It is the *dhāraṇā* (focusing on one thing) that is needed. This will gradually lead to a *dhyāna* (one-pointed concentration) and in course of time (depending on one's earlier *samskāras*) to a divine absorption (*samādhi)*. Most of us, in fact 99% of us start only this way. Very rarely great souls whose previous *samskāras* are spiritually strong (B.G. Ch.6, last six *ślokas*) start with a nirguṇa *upāsana*.

But as we (the ordinary seekers) ascend to higher levels of meditation, we must be able to orient our thoughts to think and accept that the forms of God we are meditating on are not outside, they are within us – certainly not in that physical form which we have associated with them but in their subtle formless truth, where, form, name, quality, and lilas have all merged In what we ourselves are in our Inner Self. '*sohamasmi*' – That I am – should be the goal of the perception in the mind. Of course all this has to be backed by Knowledge. The Four prerequisites (what *Ācārya Śaṅkara* stipulates) and the knowledge obtained from the *śravaṇa*-practice (listening to and hearing of upadeṣas and expositions) — all of this accompanied by a *ṣraddhā* (faith & devotion) — are assumed to be going on simultaneously, so that finally there is a conviction about the *mahāvākyās*.

But now a warning has to be given to ourselves by ourselves. We hear the statement that 'I am not the body' thousands of times. We certainly 'understand' the logic behind it. But do we 'accept' it? In fact this is the fundamental bottleneck for all spiritual practice. We understand 'I am not the body'. But we don't seem to have ever accepted it B.G. 5-13 says, '*navadvāre pure dehi, vaṣī sukham āste*'. Meaning: The Yogi 'sits' in this body of nine gates. Note the word 'sits' here. We sit in a chair or on a sofa. But have we ever used the concept 'I sit in my body'? Why don't we do this if we believe that 'I' am not the body? That is because while we consider a chair and a sofa to be distinct from us we have never 'accepted' that our body is 'distinct' from us!

Where is the source of this fault in almost all of us? It is in fact that though we do a colossal amount of '*Śravaṇam*', we never do the necessary '*Mananam*' (the chewing and the churning) of the teaching. 'I am not the body', 'I will never be the body', I was also never the body' – This thought has to sink in us through our *Mananam*. *Śravaṇa* itself must be a part of total *Mananam*. *Śravaṇam mananātmakam*, says *ācharya*. If we analyse our habits of spiritual practice it will be clear that the 'understanding' of *Vedānta* is not difficult, but it is the 'acceptance' of it that is infinitely difficult. The situation 'I am the body' has never been a fact of experience; for the 'I' has always been only a resident of the body — just as, 'I am resident in this house' is a fact of experience. All our puja, japa, vrata etc. go only up to *dhārana*, namely the focussing of the mind; but the content of the mind is never filled up with the conviction that 'I am different from the body' though the intellect is satisfied by stating it as a teaching to oneself as well as to others! It should be noted here that *Mananam* also is a kind of meditation!

The next higher stage is *Nididhyāsana*, which clears up the *viparīta - bhāvanā*, namely the *bhāvanā* that the scriptural statement of the *mahāvākyās* may not be right! The difficulty with us even at this stage, if the *viparīta bhāvana* persists, is the force of our *Vāsanas*, both gross and subtle. For example we still are obsessed with the limitations of Time and Space. Why do we say that the snake is an *adhyāsa* 'on' the rope? Where did the 'top' and 'bottom' idea come from? Only from our *vāsana* of limitations of space. When we discuss the flow of thoughts, our hand moves from left to right, to picturize the 'flow'. What is 'left' and what is 'right' here in the flow of thoughts? It is our space limitation in our mind that makes us move our hands this way!

https://youtu.be/RS_cJvRu2zc

Understanding Dharma in the Light of Advaita Philosophy

Speaker: Swamini Sadvidyananda Saraswati

While carnivorous animals have only one job of looking for food, the vegetarian animals have a second job of protecting their food. But humans have three needs – one to look for food, protect it for themselves, and most of all protect oneself from oneself (cf. B.G. Ch.6 -6). This third one comes from the fact that we have always choices to choose from. This protecting oneself from oneself is what leads to the question of *dharma*. *Dharma* is not a commandment of *Īśvara*; it is itself *Īśvara*. Because the entire material (*upādāna kāraNa)* cause for all of us and of the universe is *Īśvara*. So even as a child we know what is right and what is wrong. This minimum knowledge comes to us at birth just as a baby-monkey knows it is its own responsibility to catch full and correct hold of its mother-monkey, so that it may not fall down when the mother jumps from tree to tree.

The basic law of not doing to others what one will not like to be done for oneself by others, is known even as a child. This distinction between right and wrong is what makes *dharma* and *adharma* the opposites. *Dharma* is what requires you to make your choice to live life with minimum enjoyment. Too much enjoyment can never be had without some hurt to something else. And when invariably some hurt occurs, like for example in the daily act of cooking, that is why we have the *pancha-maha-yajñas* to nullify that feeling of a*dharma*. Note that whenever your mind is unhappy, you must have failed in following some aspect of *dharma*. Understanding *dharma* itself as *Īśvara* and the knowledge of the so-called *Advaita* would then be easy for you.

https://youtu.be/w0LC1N31J-8

Section B

Vedānta in Today's World

Is Vedānta Other-Worldly? Śaṅkara's Concept of Mithyā

Speaker: Swami Bodhananda

There is a general wrong notion among many of the western-educated Indians and also westerners that Indians in general are not interested in worldly matters, have no historical sense, don't believe in progress, and they are rather taught to suffer their pain. All this wrong notion stems from the misunderstanding of the concept of *māya* and *mithyā* which are among the key concepts of *Advaita*. *Māya* and *mithyā* are wrongly taken to mean that the world is unreal. The fundamental error in understanding these two concepts comes from not recognizing that there are three concepts of reality talked about in *Vedānta*. One is the Absolute Reality which is changeless with respect to time and space; to explain further it is unchanged and remains the same always in the three periods – past, present and future – of time. The second is the *vyāvahāric* Reality or Transactional Reality by means of which we live and operate in this world. The third is a phenomenal reality which is just the appearance of the mirror image. The last two are also clubbed together and termed *mithyā* which represents anything which in due time vanishes – like the mirror image (which vanishes almost in no time) as well as the so-called operational world and the entire universe which all certainly disappear after a period of time, though long. *Mithyā* can't stand on its own, it has to have a substratum. For the mirror image and the mirage appearance there are obvious substrata. For the universe which is also a *mithyā*, *Vedānta* says the substratum is the Absolute *Brahman* itself.

Mīyate iti māya. That is, what can be measured, is measurable, objective and can manifest or be manifested, is *māya*. In fact it is such an indeterminate that has therefore also been termed as *'anirvacanīyam'* (indeterminate). It also has alternate terms like *prakriti* (weakly translated in English as 'Nature'), *avyaktam* (unmanifest), etc. All creation and all creatures are the offshoots of *prakriti*. The eternal substratum of *prakriti* is Consciousness itself, also termed Absolute Truth, known as *Brahman*.

What *Vedāntins* condemn and therefore recommend to discard is the 'worldliness' of human beings and not the world itself. All our actions, prayers, rituals, *yajñas*, etc. have to be done in this material world only. Only the attachment to the action or the world is to be shunned off. Indians are therefore very much in this world; but as Dr. Radhakrishnan has put it, they are strongly recommended not to be 'of' the world'. You have to give up the worldliness to see *Brahman*. Worldliness includes all sense of possession and the concepts of 'Me' and 'Mine'.

Kṛṣṇa says even though he has nothing to obtain, he remains in this world and keeps on doing his duties. This is called *loka-sangraham* – a service to the world performed without any attachment or sense of doer-ship. It is in this sense that *parigraha* (sense of possession) is defaulted as a demerit. Whether it was *Śaṅkara*, or *Vyāsa* or any of the great philosophers of India there is no gain saying the fact that they were all serving the world for the betterment of the world. How can this be called unworldly?

Let us look at the criticism that Indians are taught to suffer their pain? Don't non-Indians suffer their pain? Like all the world, Indians also do turn to health-curers to alleviate their pain. There is no doubt about it. But what is special with Indians is they are taught how to bear it with patience when all alleviatory strategies and remedies fail? In such situations perhaps non-Indians curse the rest of the world for their own ills. Hindu Indians on the other hand get to know that there is a spiritual force above all other worldly forces that will certainly supersede. Since this belief is ingrained in the Indian mind, more for the restoration of the peace of mind than the alternative of living with the restlessness in the mind, the foreign criticism which does not comprehend the basic philosophy, is still going round!

Let's talk about historical sense. India has a history of more than 7000 years because they have monuments and temples that are old. They have records in the *Mahābhārata* and *Ramāyāna* which are earlier than any of the known records of history in the world. The Indian tradition is as old as the world itself and will remain as such so long as mountains and rivers exist in the world!

https://youtu.be/3Q2DfyBMyvo

Practical Application of Pancha Kośa Viveka in Everyday Life

Speaker: Shri Gokulmuthu Narayanaswamy

This is the most popular *prakriyā* (Methodology for understanding and attempting to reach the Absolute). It is very logical and systematic. There are five layers in our system of BMI.

1. Physical (Body, weight, height, colour of eyes and hair). This is common between the living being and the body which is dead just now)
2. Physiological (which comprises body temperature, pulse rate, blood pressure, sugar level, allergies, etc.) No1 and 2 are common between the living body and that which is in coma)
3. Emotional (which includes (skills, knowledge, anger, jealousy, arrogance, desire, likes and dislikes, etc.)

4. Intellectual (including Value system, ideas of right and wrong, significance of honesty and kindness, political affiliations, religious beliefs, self-discipline and self-analysis, etc.) and
5. Blissful (including one's subconscious tendencies we have brought from our past, both in this life and earlier lives)

The *sthūla-śarīra* (Material Body) is that of No.1.

The *sūkṣma* (or *linga*) *śarīra* (Subtle Body) consists of Nos.2,3, and 4

The *Karana śarīra* (the causal body) is No.5.

The *sthūla* and *sūkṣma śarīras* together constitute the *kṣara-purṣha* of 13th chapter of the *gītā*.

The *ātman-Brahman* of *Vedānta* is beyond these five. It is pure consciousness. The *Bhagavad Gītā* says you disidentify with these five layers and identify with the *ātman*. Of course this is a tall order, but that is the central point of *Vedānta*.

The five layers are called (in Sanskrit) *annamaya, prāṇamaya, manomaya, vijñānamaya* (also *buddhimaya*) and *ānandamaya kośa. Kośa* means'sheath' or 'layer'.

As far as practical *Advaita* is concerned, one should focus on what is permanent. Because Reality is beyond the five. A simple rule is to make your tendencies (*samskāras*) better than what they were the previous day by enriching your character, world-view and so forth. The purpose is to make them more long-lasting. Always note that while you have control over your upward march in spiritual ascent (because you can do the necessary corrections and *sādhana* practice), your downward match is not in your control. The slipping from any certain position will take place even without your knowing. At every layer, focus on health rather than getting obsessed with it. A healthy body is one which can be forgotten during your *sādhanās*. For that a healthy mind is also necessary. It is for that we do prayers and seek the grace of God and tutelage under a Guru. *Kaṭhopaniśad* dramatizes the whole scene by comparing your situation as seated on a chariot (BMI), your charioteer being your intellect and the horses of the chariot being your senses. The senses are only your instruments; they are not You. The charioteer is your mind which must listen to you rather than you listening to it. So turn your mind in meditation and prayer so that you can tap the Inner Bliss which is certainly there within you!

https://youtu.be/7aUNilOiXf8

Advaita in Solving Contemporary Problems

Speaker: Dr Karanam Aravinda Rao

Advaita is not a religion, like religions which mainly want to dominate. They all have commandments from one historical person to be obeyed implicitly. Advaita is an honest inquiry into Reality and tells you methods to control your mind by yourself for Inner Peace. Religion implies a social structure whereas Advaita is just a philosophy as an extension of your own personality. It accepts everyone at their own level. No talks of rewards and punishments or of blasphemy. It is an impersonal enquiry into the Truth of an infinitely existing consciousness. It accepts all traditions at various levels with their own beliefs of God. In spite of its being so liberal, egalitarian & tolerant, it is not very popular because people have not taken the required effort to understand it or there has not been enough popularization.

Though the Realisation of the Absolute and of the verifiable Ultimate Reality is the only goal, our problems are because of the prevalence of a kind of thinking which looks only at the social inequalities. The nuances, historical as well as conceptual, have either not been understood or are being misrepresented. There have been Vedic *Ṛṣis* including hundreds of woman-*Ṛṣis* called R*Ṛṣikās* who have not only contributed to our spiritual treasury but have also been *mantra-drashtas* themselves. But our *dharma śāstras* which emphasize only the do's and don'ts, are too many in number and too diverse. While propagators of various religions other than Hinduism make it a point to reach the most distant strata of society, those of Hindu religion, like the Swamis and *ācaryās*, do not have this closeness of contact with the bottom-most strata. Even those of the Hindu society who have such contacts specialize on the propagation of do's and don'ts without the support of the fundamentals of the vast scriptural foundation that speaks of the Oneness in *AdvaitaAdvaita*. This gap has to be urgently handled by our *ācaryās*. Propagation of advaitic fundamentals is the only antidote to this virus-like mischievous spread of wrong perceptions, in our most ancient universe of *Sanātana Dharma*.

https://youtu.be/pCGwfd8lnmY

Need for Vedānta in Everyone's Life

Speaker: Swami Brahmavidananda

Swamiji cited a number of examples of persons seeking his advice for problems in their life. Whether rich or poor, socially at high level or not, man or woman, married or single, young or old, scripturally oriented or not - all of them, after an intense discussion, express their sense of unfulfilment, some of them because of unhappiness but most of them, in spite of their happy life. This non-fulfilment is not because of any material insufficiency of property, wealth or circumstances. But it is a feeling from the heart – like, absence of satisfaction heart wise. It is a need of the heart. It comes from the heart. It is a feeling of being limited from the heart. All our actions are in time and space, therefore certainly limited. This universal human need for fulfilment, i.e. for a limitless fulfilment (not in terms of material desires, but it is more subtle than that) is what needs the *Vedānta* for its antidote & release. Only *Vedānta* can solve this. The common prerequisites of discretion and dispassion are the preliminaries to understand this *Vedāntic* answer. Advaita is not for the other world. In this life itself we know many things, but we usually don't live by what we know. *Vedānta* is for the management of desires so that the emptiness of non-fulfilment is handled properly.

https://youtu.be/dUrjqVZekTQ

Advaitic Teachings on Titikṣā: How to Deal with Ups & Downs of Life

Speaker: Shri N Venkatraman

Ādi Śaṅkara, in whose name we are celebrating this global festival - his very name sends a thrill in our veins because of his infinite *Titikṣā* (Patience and forbearance) in unifying many spiritual aspirations of varying and conflicting opinions in the land and bringing most of them under one umbrella of Oneness by sheer patient talks and discussions with them. In today's impatient world, we have to learn and practice that *Titikṣā* which he displayed so successfully. You may ask now: Why do we need to be patient when the rest of the world is restless and competing to be one up all the time. Whatever the common opinion may be, it cannot be denied that all those across the world who have had excellent performances to their credit either in personal life or scientific life or spiritual life, have shown enormous patience. They had the passion and the unflinching oneness of purpose to achieve what they achieved. We ordinary common folk have first to acquire patience as our foremost quality. A patient person generally tends to be positive. There are three common areas where patience is most invaluable: One is the series of routine irritations that we certainly meet in our life's journey. The second is the certain-to-arrive uncouth situations and failure of efforts. The third is the handling of emotional setbacks in human relations. If you lose patience you lose the battle. If you happen to be in a leading position either in a team or in the official hierarchy, an impatient leader can never be a leader, because he will lose any trust that was already placed in him. Patience implies a sort of stress no doubt; for things can go wrong in spite of your best efforts. That is the time when you have to bring your power of *Titikṣā*

Most of all patience invites what is usually styled as suffering. But you have to cultivate the habit of suffering your losses, either material or non-material. As human beings, whether in ordinary practice of living our life or in the *sādhana* of spiritual training, the ability to control the senses over a natural impatience that is bound to arise is what transforms your patience into forbearance. You cannot afford to lose your power of endurance. There is an inner strength, according to *Sanatana Dharma*, which will help you tide over the onslaught of impatience. God helps those who help themselves with vigilance and hard work. The B.G. has almost the final word on this. *Daivī sampat vimokṣaya*, says ch.16. And what is *daivī sampat*? The important qualities that are included in it are: *dama* (control of senses); *kṣamā* (patience); *dhritih* (fortitude) and *śānti* (tranquillity). These four are the ones which add up to the covetable quality of *Titikṣā*.

https://youtu.be/MxIUkyQ70w0

Bhagavadgītā: Self-Management - Success Redefined

Speaker: Shri Krishnaphani Kesiraju

We look at *Śaṅkara bhāṣya* of B.G. from a new perspective, namely, Self-Management, a most neglected aspect acc. to the speaker. First seven pairs of words are culled out from the *bhāṣya* itself. They are:

Pravrritti (outward acquisition) and *Nivritt*i (Inward renunciation. Both are required for self-management.

Abhyudaya (Worldly prosperity) and *niśreyasa* (Emancipation)

Svabhāva (Innate Nature) and *Svadharma* (Duty and Responsibility) The first is individualised but also being evolved in course of time; the second is a function of class, station and situation. These have optimal advantages for a spiritual unfoldment. Anything which rebels against the *svabhava* is *paradharma*. *Svabhāva* and *svadharma* together constitute an endless cycle (which is therefore circular, with no beginning, no end). So what you have to do for self-management acc. to B.G's *Karma yoga* is to move in a perpendicular direction to the plane of the circle! It has to be a 'vertical' take-off along the *jñāna* path.

Avidyā (nescience) and *kāma* (Desire). These are the ones which give rise to the concepts of 'I' and 'Mine' and also *rāga* and *dvesha* – the root of all actions. For a discerning man (*viveki*) neither of these gives pleasure, because they end in sorrow

Śoka (Grief and sorrow) and *moha* (Delusion and Bewilderment), these two separate you from Happiness.

Sānkhya (Discrimination-based *yoga*) and *Karma* (*Yoga* of Action). The latter originates from Ignorance and Detachment, the purpose being *ātma-śuddhi*.

The commentaries of *Bhagavatpāda* to be referred are: II-11.0 (for the Absolute); II -39.1 for true nature of the Absolute; III-3.1 for Self and non-self; III-3.1 for the steadiness in *ātma-*

jñāna and IV-5 for *ātma-śuddhi*. And III-4.2 and V-11 for *Karma Yoga* inner concept.

Yoga and *kshema* (II -45 and IX – 22)

And then the seven dimensions of success, not to be taken as worldly success are:

Sahaja which is nothing but the inherent *svabhāva; Sarala* which simplifies one's life; *Svastha,* which is stability in oneself also from the spiritual angle (III-17, VI-5 and VI-20); *Saphala* which is fruition, not success; for action predetermines result; *Samriddhi* (II-71): which is the Perfection of (III -20, 25); *Sampanna*: which is the excellence of completion

https://youtu.be/gt4haNeUqgk

Vedānta & Psychology - Śaṅkara's Upadeṣa Sāhasrī

Speaker: Swamini Brahmaprajnananda Saraswati

The popular doubt always is: If I am *Brahman*, why don't I feel it? To explain this we may go to the 19th chapter of the *padya* portion of *Upadeṣa Sāhasrī* of *Śaṅkara*. In this chapter there is an imaginary talk between the Self (*ātman*) and the Mind! Let us listen to the *ātman* speaking to the Mind:

Remember, you Mind, you have no independent existence of your own. It is important to listen to the Guru's *upadeṣas* and churn them out yourself and finally meditate on the findings. On the other hand always you feel isolated though you want to acquire enlightenment. I am all-pervading. But because of your ideas of I-ness (*ahamkara*) and my-ness (*mamakāra*), you are afraid to recognise my presence. You, Mind, is only an object (*driśyam* - seen). I am the *drik* (Seer).

I am formless and attribute-less. My bliss is ever flowing. But you are subject to modifications (*vrittis*). I am beyond all the three *guṇas*. Also I am the *sākṣī* of all the three states of Waking, Dream and Sleep. You are constantly occupied by thoughts; but what is there between two thoughts of yours? You don't seem to recognise that that is where I am! In each and every cognition of yours – for example, 'the chair is…', 'the laptop is …', 'the book is …'., In each of these cognitions of yours, I am the 'is-ness'. I am ever free and complete. Everything exists in Me. I don't need you at all. Nor do I have to relax, like you! You want to relax from your worries, because, you need fulfilment. I don't need any fulfilment because I am fulfilled. I am the Ocean and you are the wave but your content is only Water, that is, Me. You are so much mistaken, and therefore you suffer; Relax and recognize Me (and nothing else) as your substratum Analyse you experiences; but I, *Brahman*, that you are, is not an experience. It is the One and only one ultimate fact and wisdom!

https://youtu.be/yCFW98kDBrI

Science and Vedānta

Speaker: Acharya Kuntimaddi Sadananda

There are three things for knowledge to arise – either in Science or in *Vedānta*. It is *pramātā*, the knower; *prameya,* the known and *pramāṇa*, the means of connecting the two.

Three methods for the knowledge to arise – either in Science or in *Vedānta*. It is *pratyakṣa* i.e. direct perception (either human perception or instrument perception); *anumāna* i.e. logical deduction or induction; and three, the *shabda*, i.e. through a reliable source.

Direct perceptive knowledge may be of two kinds:

1. I see it, therefore it is there; and
2. It is there, therefore I see it.

Sometimes a later perception (recall the 'snake and the rope' analogy) may deny the validity of the earlier perception, as in the case of all illusive perceptions so that what was a *pramā* (perceptive truth) earlier becomes a *bhramā* (illusion) later.

Anumāna also is of two kinds: one, worldwide routine; and two: depending on *śabda - pramāṇa* like the knowledge of heaven and hell.

Suppose I am in a dark room. Somebody from outside asks "Is there a chair there?" I cannot answer the question because I can't see in the dark. But suppose he asks: Are you there? I don't need any help to answer this. For I know that I am there; the fact 'I am' is self-evident, because I am a self-existing, self-conscious being. I don't need any *pramāṇa* (means of knowledge) for this knowledge. Now *Vedānta* says: Not only are you self-evident and self-existing; but you are also truly infinite. Here *Vedānta* becomes a *pramāṇa* (means).

Now let us question: 'How do I know my room is dark? Because I am myself the Light of Consciousness (which is what I am, according to *Vedānta*).

Let us analyse the two statements 'I am' and 'I exist'. The question that *Vedānta* asks is: Who is this 'I' in the statement 'I am'? You cannot answer it by giving all details of your profile. *Vedānta* very deftly makes a distinction between 'What you are' and 'What you think you are'. The subject of 'I am' cannot be objectified. Anything that can be objectified cannot be the 'I' or 'me'. The cognitive scientists explore the objects called 'mind' and 'brain' but can never explore the 'subject' itself. Science can deal only with objectifiable things.

Vedānta uses the indicative definition of its mantra 7 (*nāntah prajnam,* etc. in *Māṇḍūkya Upaniṣad*) to analyse this 'I'. They tell you who you are by negating all the things you are not. This kind of indicator definition makes you jump to 'mind' and 'brain'. When I see an object, actually what I see is the quantum of reflections of the light from the object into my brain, where the neurons have programmed, (by God probably!) method by which they are converted into a 'thought' for the mind; this is how we 'perceive' an object. So all knowledge requires a mind – which registers the light of consciousness on the thought generated by the neurons in the brain. And *Vedānta* says this un-objectifiable 'I' is nothing but the vastness of *Brahman*. In other words 'I' is infinite.

Does it mean that there are as many infinites as there are individuals? No. Because two infinites, in other words, two things which are both unlimited, cannot exist, for each will limit the other. In fact, the 'I' which is the infinite Consciousness is also transcending Time and Space. Time is what transpires between two sequential experiences (happenings) and Space is what exists between two simultaneous experiences. So neither time nor space is meaningful in an Infinite Consciousness, because this Infinite is one and only one. *Ekam-eva-advitīyam-brahma*!

https://youtu.be/lkuEhnh1Az8

Vedānta & Modern Mindfulness

Speaker: Shri Kathirasan K

"Mindfulness is awareness that arises through paying attention, on purpose, in the present moment, non-judgmentally, in the service of self-understanding and wisdom", Dr Jon Kabat-Zinn Ph.D. Professor of Medicine Emeritus, University of Massachusetts Medical School.

Two Mechanisms of Mindfulness Meditation

1. Focused Attention - voluntary focusing attention on a chosen object in a sustained fashion
2. Open Monitoring - non-reactive monitoring of the content of experience from moment to moment, primarily as a means to recognize the nature of emotional and cognitive patterns.

Seven attitudes

- Non- Judging

- Patience
- Beginner's Mind
- Trust
- Non-Striving
- Acceptance
- Letting Go

Practices: Sitting Meditation, Loving Kindness Meditation, Walking Meditation, Body Scan, Mindful *Yoga*. Mindful Eating, Awareness of Breath.

Philosophy of the Self

1. "Although our patients all come with various problems, diagnoses, and ailments, we make every effort to apprehend their intrinsic wholeness" (Kabat-Zinn, 2011, p.292)
2. "We are also what was present before the scarring— our original wholeness, what was born whole. And we can reconnect with that intrinsic wholeness at any time, because its very nature is that it is always present. It is who we truly are." (Kabat-Zinn, 2013, p.185) 3. "When we are in touch with being whole, we feel at one with everything. When we feel at one

with everything, we feel whole ourselves" (Kabat-Zinn): 1994, p.226

1. Two ideas emerge from these statements:
    - Wholeness is intrinsic
    - Wholeness is non-dual
2. Ideas of wholeness were not taught in early Buddhism. Modern mindfulness adopts a life-positive approach compared to a pessimistic approach
3. Ideas of Wholeness are presented in the *Upaniṣad-s* as *pūrna* or ananta (*pūrna* - BU 5.1.1; BG 8.4, 8.22; ananta - TU 2.1.1; BS 3.2.37; CU 3.14.1)
4. The Non-duality alluded is an idea similar to *Advaita Vedānta* teachings

https://youtu.be/Ib8Pqs8hr-4

Sādhana on the Path of Advaita in the Modern Context

Speaker: Shri Chittaranjan Naik

What is the goal of *Advaita sādhana*? *mokṣa*. And what is *mokṣa*? It is Self-Realisation – beyond speech and thought. We can't ever specify it as this or that. If it is so unspecifiable and unknowable, how can we be attached to it? It is something which cannot be spoken of; still it is the goal. Here is a simple parallel. A King is living in a palatial palace with all his riches, all wants satisfied and he has never gone out of his palace nor has he any windows to look out. What lies outside as the world is totally unknown to him. He can think of it only as a void. In Plato's Republic, he describes a situation as follows. We are all in a cave in which we can see only the walls. Outside people cast shadows on the wall. Anyone who goes out is blinded by sunlight and comes back and has nothing to tell anybody anything worthwhile. These two examples are excellent analogies for what we understand about *mokṣa*! Then what makes an advaitin need *mokṣa*? B.G. 2.57 says even when you withdraw from sense objects, the taste remains until you have tasted the Supreme. So the key factor is you have to lose the taste of what all you know and have experienced!

This is what is meant by the word *'atha'*, the very first word in the first *Brahmasūtra*. *Śaṅkara* says you need the four qualifications before you can go for the taste of the supreme. They are discrimination, dispassion, set of six qualities like *śama*, *dama* etc. and finally *mumukṣutvam* which is an irrevocable one-pointed objective of *mokṣa*. The *Bhāgavatam* gives a beautiful analogy. If the water of the lake is foggy and turbulent you can't see any reflection. The water has to be calm and clear. In the same way your mind has to be crystal-pure. Otherwise Knowledge of the Self is out of the question. But the Self is never unknown. It is *svayamprakāśa*. It illuminates itself to everyone. So the problem is our mind.

Two types are recognised: *pravritti* and *nivritti*. The latter is that of renunciation of actions. But the path itself is *śravaṇa*, *manana* and *nidhidhyāsana*. The rise of spiritual fire from within is the recognition that every cognition rises from the Self. This spark from within is called *pratyabhijnā*. *Māya* covers it, but *Vidya* uncovers it. Even a *madhyamādhikāri* (one who is not fully qualified with the four prerequisites) gets the chance to abide in the Self (*Nididhyāsana*) by doing the *manana* constantly. It is the *manana* that drives away all your doubts (*samśayās*). The final stage is not an attainment, because you are already 'It'; so what you have at the final stage is the recognition that you are the Self. It is an effortless re-cognition. In B.G. *Kṛṣṇa* dissuades *Arjuna* from renunciation, because *Arjuna*, according to *Kṛṣṇa*, is not yet ready for it. By doing the obligatory duties without attachment (this is *pravritti*) (and renouncing the *kāmya karmās*) one gets the mental purity that will lead to the goal through the *sādhana* of *manana* and *nididhyāsana* and this leads you to a mental *nivritti* and this is the penultimate stage of the recognition of the Self.

https://youtu.be/XKqFCKU-DQ

In Pursuit of Happiness – Insights from Advaita Vedānta

Speaker: Prof. B Mahadevan

First please note the difference between 'In search of Happiness' and 'In Pursuit of happiness'. The Advaita teaching is: you don't search for happiness; it is already in you. What we all do is to 'pursue' happiness, thinking that it is outside us. In this there is a western perspective which always looks for self-enhancement so that one can be at the top of the world. We unfortunately mainly draw from that perspective. On the other hand, the eastern perspective emphasizes self-transcendence, which is non-ephemeral and recommends a life of harmony rather than one-up-manship. In order to understand this better, we have to look at *Vedānta*, in which everything is embodied with happiness. Not only humans, certainly animals, but even so-called inert objects like trees and mountains. Once we understand that the idea of happiness is also there for plants and trees, our very concept of ecology will change. The *ānanda* that *Upaniṣads* talk about is not the limited health-wealth-centred enjoyment called pleasure and happiness, but what they talk about is a universally inherent attribute in everything. *ānanda* according to *Vedānta* is in us 24 x7.

But our personal experiences seem to say something else, totally contrary. But we do experience total bliss when we are in deep sleep. And this we all do daily. Then why is it evading us during our waking time? *Advaita* is clear that it is because of our non-experience of *Advaita*. We cry from the housetop that there is only Oneness (non-duality) all around but we don't practise it. Remember sleep never bores us; in fact when we are bored we want to go to sleep. Sleep is the state when *prakriti* takes us in her lap and recharges us, so that we say the next day: 'Oh, I had a good sleep, I slept happily!'. Let us begin to see the world as One and one only. In other words, see the world through the advaitic lens. As *Śaṅkara* very emphatically starts his *adhyāsa bhāṣya*, saying that it is the difference between the concepts of 'I' (*asmat*) and 'you' (*yuṣmat*) that we entertain is the fundamental exhibition of our age-old Ignorance. This difference, namely between the world (*viṣaya*) and ourselves (*viṣayī*) is the *bhedabhāva*, the attitude of separateness that prevents the *Brahmabhāva* that ought to be with us. This *bhedabhāva* is what makes us go after *kośānanda* (happiness that comes from the material modes of existence) and not *ātmananda* (bliss that is inherent in Self-realisation). We are confused between the original and its reflection. World is full of reflections only. Any happiness that we experience lasts only so far as we do not see something better. Pure Joy or Bliss is totally different from what we mean by enjoyment, which is only an experience of the *indriyās*. Success is not happiness. Happiness is beyond Success. So we have to refocus our attitudes. Instead of revolving around perishable happiness we should look for the non-perishable. *Śaṅkara,* therefore has a magical recommendation: Invest in *vairāgya* (dispassion, detachment). That will divert you onto the right road to Knowledge, and Eternal Peace which is the limitless Happiness.

https://youtu.be/yUvsGw8BXbs

The Relevance of Vedānta to Western Seekers

Speaker: Sadhvi Tilakaa Tatiane Barcelos

There are two kinds of western seekers. The first group doesn't value these scriptures and they ask: How do you know they are speaking the truth? It is all blind belief and old school thinking according to them. The second group has had some contact with Indian *Vedānta* teachers like bhajan groups, Hare *Kṛṣṇa* devotees and various Swami jis. But even this second group has a standard question: Can't we know all this from the books? Why do I have to listen to teachers? The second group even overshoots us by declaring: 'We have our Inner Guru; why do we need an outside guru?'!

Both the groups have to realise that the purpose of *Vedānta* is to tell you that there is a reality (*kevalah*) which you have to realise here and now. *Kevalasya bhāvah kaivalyam*, meaning *mokṣa* (release from transmigration, namely births and further births). The relevance of *Vedānta* is because it is the means to *mokṣa*. The preliminary prayer to Dakṣiṇāmūrti says he the almighty is the Doctor for the illness of *samsāra* (*bhiṣaje bhava rogiṇām).*

This body-mind complex is only *kārya-karāṇa-sanghāta* (acc. to *Ācārya Śaṅkara*), meaning, a complex of cause and effect. B. G. 13-1.2 says that everything is *kṣetra* (field) and the One who is the Seer-Knower of this *kṣetra* is the Supreme (*kṣetrajna*). This implies that *Īśvara* is everything and is everywhere. (Not physically inside: medical investigation will not reveal it). This knowledge is *samyak-jñāna* (well-rounded knowledge). There is nothing other than the Supreme. Śaṅkara uses powerful words in his *bhāṣya*: *tasya vyatirekeNa anyad nāsti* – Other than Him, there is nothing else. This knowledge is so fundamental that *Nārada* learns from *Sanatkumāra* (Ch.U.7-1-3) that the knower of the Self (*Brahman*) transcends all sorrows (*tarati shokam ātmavit*). All of us are under a misconception (*bhrānti*). *Samyak-darshanam* (Appropriate perception) is what is needed. (*Śaṅkara bhāṣya*M of B.G. 6-37). *Jnānād eva kaivalyam* says *Garuda purāṇa* of *Vyasa*

(2-49-87). This *jñāna* that we are talking about is not a bunch of words and their meaning. The unique word *mantra* means the knowledge is inbuilt into the words. And that knowledge takes you out of your *śoka* (sorrow of non-fulfilment). Oh God, I am sad, afflicted, please make me cross over this (Ch.U.7-23-1). And it declares what is Infinite and Limitless (*bhūmā*) is Happiness; what is finite is otherwise. That is the One to be investigated and learnt by special efforts (*visheshheṇa vijnāsitavyam*)

The standard question comes again: Why can't I know it myself. *Yamadharma Rāja* answers in *Kaṭhopaniṣad*: The senses are condemned to look only outside and never inside; Only a rare person looks inside. "*parāmchi khāni.. kashcid dhīrah..* Katha U. 2-1-1). Be that rare '*dhīra*'.

Mundakopaniṣad clarifies further. There are two kinds of Knowledge, *parā* and *aparā*. The latter tells you about *akṣaram*. *Na kṣarati iti akṣaram*, that is, what does not change is *akṣaram*, the Imperishable. B.G. 8-3 declares that this *akṣara* is the supreme *Brahman*. *Mundaka Upaniṣad*: *Brahma veda Brahma eva bhavati* (3-2-9). One who knows *Brahman*, 'becomes' *Brahman*. This 'becoming' is actually a wrong word (Recall *Taittitīya Upaniṣad: yato vāco nivartante*: From which words retreat!); because the root verb; *bhū'* here does not mean 'becomes' but means just 'be'. In other words, He who knows *Brahman* is *Brahman*. *Brahman* is one who sustains all existences and all kinds of activities (*Brahmasūtra bhāṣya* to 1-8). That *Brahman* is *apūrvam* (no beginning) *anaparam* (no end) *anantaram* (no inside) *abāhyam* (no outside) (Br.U. 2-5-19). This is the teaching (*anushāsanam*). So *Uddalaka* tells *Svetaketu* that this Self is *Brahman* (*ayamātmā Brahman*).

Thus *Vedānta* is the only authority (*pramāṇa*) for this knowledge. So it is *pramāṇa* the means (*pramā karāṇam pramāṇam*). This is in *Vedānta Sāra*, a *prakaraṇa grantha*. And *Vedānta Sāra* continues that the *adhikar*i (the executive, the right one) is *pramātā* (the teacher.) He must have been equipped with the four-fold prerequisites *(sādhana catuṣṭaya* of *Śaṅkara*). *Tad-vijnānārtham gurumevā gacchet śrotriyam Brahmaniśṭham* (Mu.U.1-2-12). In order to know this you have to go to a qualified, well-read, *Brahmaniśṭha*. And you have to have both *śraddhā* and *bhakti*, *yathā deve tathā gurau*

(As in God so in the Guru). Only he, one who has *śraddhā* the incessant urge to go forward with faith and devotion (B.G. 4-39) will get the *jñānam*. What does one get after that: Absolute Peace (*parā shānti).* And what is this *jñāna*? It is the Oneness of *jīva* and *Brahman*. Once the assumed difference between *jīva* and *Brahman* is negated the *samsāra* is crossed. (*bhedapratipatteh samsāragamanm* – *Upadeṣa Sāhasri*, 27, 28) And *Īśopaniśad* declares 'where is the delusion or misery for one who thus realises the Reality?' ('*anupaśyatam*' is the word used by *Īśopaniśad*).

https://youtu.be/PkuavTQIwHo

Vedānta for Youths

Speaker: Shri P Lakshminarayanan

The youth is well-known for its exuberance and vigour. But as we nurture a sapling for it to grow as a useful plant or tree, we have to give direction to the youth even around the ages of 6 or 7 or 8, because that is the best time to train the intellect. If the intellect is not properly trained, the human being becomes almost an animal. *Panchadaśi* has a *śloka* which says *dharma* is the difference between a human being and an animal; but more than that one may say it is the thinking habit that is what makes a human being different. Animals in Tamil are called *'kālnadai'*, meaning that they walk with their feet and do nothing else, whereas we walk with our feet but also 'think'. That is why in Sanskrit a human being is called a '*manuśya*' the word coming from the root verb '*man*' to think. A human being is therefore an animal plus higher values and awareness. We are only 'evolved' animals. All the bad things in the universe are mostly man's doing; for example, global warming. We have to be governed; if not, we function as an animal!.

It is the *śruti* (*Vedas* and *Upaniṣads*) through its *Vedānta* that provides us the technique of living. If we get lost in a dense forest without any means of communication with the outside world like cell phones etc., the only way we can find our directions is by looking at the Sun, its position and its movement. It is *Vedānta* that directs us in this dense forest of life. *Vedānta* is the collective experience of all the wise sages put into our *śāstras*. They tell us our physical dynamics of work, the emotional calmness of mind that is necessary, and the original thinking for the intellect. They do this through an unending spirit of questioning. They encourage every kind of questioning. They even question the very existence of the universe we see around us. Questions like 'What and Why', 'When and How', 'Where and Who' – all inculcate the human thinking habit into right directions. Certainly these important questions are also handled by our Science and worldly education. But the most essential questions are handled by *Vedānta* only.

B. G. rightly says that thoughts (*dhyāyato viṣayān…*) indiscriminately dwell on sense objects and this is what ultimately spoils us. We ourselves are responsible for our purposeful growth (Ch.6 – 6 of B.G.) Rightly does Arjuna ask questions about the intractability of the mind which behaves like a monkey. Only when you can control your mind you can be successful. Even in a sport like cricket, as a batsman when you receive a ball, you have to decide beforehand whether you have to use your usual tendency to hit a cover drive or not. In that sense the mind has to be in your control all the time.

Thoughts create our Destiny. Because thoughts to words to actions to repeated actions to habit to destiny — this is an age-old chain of human behaviour. This is how our *samskāras* (tendencies) shape up. As you think so you reap. Even when cooking your food, if you do not share it with the needy at your door, you are only a '*stena*' (meaning 'thief'), says the *Veda*. The thought quality has to be transformed from 'Me' and 'Mine' to a broader vision. Mind and Ego are the basic culprits. All our problems, like stress etc. are from within us, not outside. This is one of the greatest lessons that youth has to learn from

Vedānta. The youth even as a youth should start studying the scriptures to sharpen the mind and steer it in the right direction which helps not only him or her but also the rest of the world. Don't accept anything for granted; think. An idle mind is a devil's workshop. Keep physically active; Sleep neither excessively nor very little. All this constitutes the art of self-management.

https://youtu.be/0rSFaAQWSAs

Transcending Hate through Advaita

Speaker: Shri R S Ravi

This is a talk which might be useful to both kinds of people – namely, those who are already on the spiritual path as well as those who are only fence-sitters who have not yet made up their mind to choose the spiritual path.

First, what is hatred or hate? A mild form of it is 'disliking'. *Dveśa* is the Sanskrit word which indicates the more intense form. The root cause of it all is mostly the age-old *vāsanas*. Is there any way to substantiate this statement that it is an age-old *vāsana* effect? Yes, there is. Watch any pair of twins. Mostly you will find their attributes differ – in spite of the fact that they were born from the same womb for the same parents almost at the same time. Also when you do not like something even while young, if the same object happens to be thrust on you repeatedly your original mild dislike becomes a hatred for the object. Another way in which dislike grows into hatred even when you are a grown up adult may be the job surrounding you is disliked by you and in due time it becomes hatred for either the boss or for the job itself.

What does *Advaita* say? A person having *rāga* and *dveśa* – attachment and hate – is actually committing a sin. Hatred is nothing but accumulation of what is called '*pāpa*' in *Sanātana Dharma*. The purpose of this rare (*durlabham*) birth as a human being is Liberation – in fact, liberation here and now as a *jīvan-mukta*. *Vedānta* is generally interested in your mental condition, more than your external actions. Still it says (*Bhaja Govindaṃ*) "*mūdha jahīhi dhanāgama trishhṇām*". If you do not care for this, you are already on the downward path! This is the first dimension of *Advaita* regarding the concept of hate.

The second dimension is the pervasion of Absolute Consciousness in the entire Universe. The transactional world (which is *mithyā*) is only for transactional purposes. So the *Sanatana Dharma* charts out a road map for you to keep your mind free, contented and fulfilled. There are three steps in this.

First step is ethical living. You have to make this as a starting point, with no compromise made. What you do not want to happen for you should not be done for others. This is a beautiful blend of individual ethics and societal ethics. Contentment will be there so long as you do not compare with others and so long as no jealousy develops in the interior of the mind. Make your best efforts. Keep your best foot forward. And don't compare.

Second step. Believe in the invisible fate of *prārabdha*. If it is unhelpful, try to distinguish between choice-ful actions and choice-less actions. *gītā* (2-27) says '*aparihāryārthe na* tv*am ṣocitum arhasi*". Again it also says *'Titikṣāsva'*. What you cannot overcome you have to accept – with grace, not ill will or hatred. God is always there. There is no spirituality without religion.

So the third step is a mind which is ready to offer everything to the almighty (B.G.9-27). This *samarpaṇa buddhi* is the ultimate antidote for all feelings of unfulfilment. Emotional support will always be there for one who is able to offer everything (both positive and negative happenings) to the Lord. There are stories where one driving to the airport is stuck up with traffic jams and so will definitely miss one's flight, but as one goes along driving and praying to the Lord intensely, later finds that even the pilot of the particular flight was also locked up in the same traffic jam and so finally one gets into the intended flight!

https://youtu.be/KNgUveNDisQ

Practising Advaita Sādhana: Benefits & Challenges

Speaker: Shri Ramesh Venkatraman

Even as a boy of eight years or so, knocking at the cave of the would-be *Guru Govindapāda*, Śaṅkara declared in his *Daṣashlokī* that he was neither the elements nor anything of this universe but he was *ṣivah kevalah* – the One indivisible Self. This is the goal of all *Advaita* – to realise the universality of the Self and its Oneness. The *jivātma-paramātma* identity is almost like a droplet of water merging into a glass of water. But our infinite number of attractions and distractions in the visible world hide our vision. They say this is the effect of *māya*. Do we generally accept it? Is it easy to convince ourselves this is so? What we need is freedom from our own mind. Swami Vivekānanda says: Keep asking questions. You will know. Even *Nārada* in Chāndogya Upaniṣad could not accept it when *Sanatkumāra* told him the nature of *Brahman*. Where is the *Brahman*'s support, asks *Nārada* (*kasmin pratiṣtitah*). And the answer comes: It is *sve mahimni*, i.e. on its own Power. And finally *Sanatkumāra* says, Maybe I don't know; in the style of the *Nasadīya suktam* of *Ṛgveda*.

Today there are easier accesses to get that teaching. We have real stories from people who lived in our memory, like Shri Ramakrishna. Standing on the banks of the Ganga, he sees two boats are fighting with each other in which one boatman gave a severe blow to the other boatman. Ramakrishna With his universal Consciousness watching it, felt the blow on his own self, to such an extent that others could even see the mark on his chest. This kind of Oneness with the Universe is a rare fortune to witness. Paul Brunton when he visited *Ramaṇa* could not ask even a single question verbally; but as every question passed through his mind, the answer also flashed in his mind from the sage! To some westerner who would not accept all the intricacies of the philosophy, but who asked the question of *Ramaṇa*, whether by repeating the name of *Nārāyaṇa* he can go to Vaikuntha, see God *Viṣṇu* and talk to Him and what *Viṣṇu* would say to him, *Ramaṇa Mahaṛṣi* replies in his characteristic style: "Yes, He would ask you to find out who you are"!

All this is interesting. But the mind has its own ways. As *Kānchi Mahāswamigal* said, the bundled up mind has no freedom from its thoughts and emotions which perennially make you struggle with them and so the job of freeing the mind from the thoughts is as difficult as, if not more than, taking off not just your tight shirt, but even the skin off you. Says he: "Mind is a machine that constantly generates thoughts and it behaves like a proverbial monkey which is not only intoxicated, but also bitten by a scorpion"! And *Kṛṣṇa* himself agrees with *Arjuna* when the latter cites the impossibility of getting freedom from the mind. Most of us have a mild relationship with the Almighty only in the process of *ṣaraṇāgati*, not in the process of understanding His opulence. But surprisingly we have even recent historical examples like a *Sadāṣiva Brahmendra* who may be said to be the most thorough instance of a *jīvanmukta* who cared just zero percent for any of the material pulls but always lived and roamed about in the fullness of the Infinite.

For us, ordinary people, between the *sat* (Existence) and *ānanda* (Bliss), there is our individual *cit* (instead of the universal *cit*) that stands in the middle and prevents our transcending the mind. Mind is a great master and we are poor slaves before it. The much-talked about liberation is not the light at the end of the tunnel. My own personal method (says the speaker) is not to spend any more time on keeping on studying and trying to learn, but to do the *sādhana* of every single name from the *Viṣṇu Sahasranāma*, one every day, and do the *sādhana* of the mind revolving around all the intricate meanings of that one name for that day! The so-called *māya* is an Entanglement from which there is no release except by such eternal *sādhanas*. You cannot have scientific validation of all these. Would science accept a philosophical validation of its scientific fundamentals? The appeal, the applicability and usefulness of our *sādhanas* can never be validated by science or any other gadget; it has its authority only by experience!

https://youtu.be/ULVB56WFxso

How Vedānta Helps One to Live a Meaningful Life

Speaker: Shri Karthikeyan Laxman

Having got an invaluable rare human life because of various past *karmās*, we have to go through life, the journey being one of snakes and ladders. Scriptures give you four objectives. The fourth *puruṣartha*, which is liberation from this repeated transmigration, assures us Peace, Security and Happiness as an eternal benefit. On the other hand life in this world shows us beauty, variety and novelty but with no stability. So we look for ways and means to lead a meaningful life that will take us on to that fourth *puruṣartha*, namely *mokṣa*. There are seven must-be-followed living commandments

Always lead an ethical life. The thumb rule is: 'Do not do unto others what you do not want to be done to yourself'. Both at the individual level and at the social level, this has to be followed.

Lead a life of contribution to the world rather than counting on what you will get from the world: We usually take from Nature more than what we receive from it; in fact this is the major cause for many of the problems with our ecosystem. Also with the rest of mankind we have to contribute with money, wealth and knowledge. Lord *Kṛṣṇa* rightly pinpoints this as *yajña, dāna, tapah* – the three duties in which we should not make any compromise.

Lead a prayerful life. Only by prayers to *Īśvara* do we show our gratitude to whatever we receive. By prayers we substantially reduce the turbulence in the mind. We all have a large bundle of negatives (*pāpa* balance) in our *karma*-bank account which is of two kinds, *prārabdha* and *sancita.* We should keep on trying to improve the *punya* balance in this account. The *bhaja-govindam śloka* '*geyam gītā-namasahasram.*' gives us the two fold recharger of our energies in the form of self-effort as well as God's Grace.

Lead a life of moderation with respect to food, recreation, in fact with respect to all our involvements. This conserves and nurtures our mental energy. The simple strategy is not to get addicted to anything.

Channelize all your ten sense organs in the right directions constantly raising the divine inspired aspirations. The chariot of the body is to be piloted by the intellect so that the horses-like senses do not take you into excessive indulgence in wrong avenues. But do not forcibly suppress the desires. It is the channelization that is more important than the struggle with desires.

Develop the sense of equanimity with respect to objects, with respect to people and with respect to all happenings to you. This is the most difficult requirement, of course. But without this *sama-darśanam*, nothing good can be achieved. *Kṛṣṇa* emphasises this more than once in the B.G. When you have the choice, follow all the above rules. When you do not have a choice, develop the mood of acceptance as God's will! (as in the *apariharyārthe*… *śloka* in the *gītā* II-27). Equanimity is the first step to spirituality. The frequency and intensity with which you can observe equanimity will decide how quickly you can recover from the unacceptable tendencies which may be already ingrained in you by your own past.

This is the road map for *cittaśuddhi* (Purification of mind) and one-pointedness (*ekāgratā*) towards the ultimate goal. Once you are on this route, it will take you as if, through a divine escalator (Ch.6 of B.G), to the desired deserving goals of life.

https://youtu.be/zsQgcW6ynO0

Significance of Vedānta in Daily Life

Speaker: Shri Krishnan Subramanian

Vedānta is subjective; Science is objective. *Vedānta* occupies itself with people, who generally handle the same situation in different ways. It declares self-mastery as the ultimate victory; because everything of interest to *Vedānta* happens in the mind. *Vedānta* considers material happenings as trivial. It constantly reminds us: '*ātmavān bhava*'. But the fundamental problem that it presents to each individual is: "can I create a space between me and my mind?" *Bhagavad gītā* (B.G.) says *Vedānta* is your daily life. But the public understanding of *Vedānta* is built around several myths.

MYTH 1: '*Vedānta* is for old people'. No it is not. For, look at the simple happening. We all take health insurance because we want to be able to confront all issues of ill-health. Do we make any preventive measures for the prevention or confrontation of emotional issues? Swami Chinmayananda used to comment: 'I want to see more youth in my audience'. *Vedānta* is not only for old people. '*bālastāvat krīdāsaktah* ...' says Bhaja Govindam. The problem of daily life is there for all. The *Vedas* and *Vedānta* constitute an excellent user manual for living. The time for the use of the manual is now, not after sixty.

MYTH 2: 'Spirituality means *Sannyāsa*'. Not at all. Read ch.4 and 5 of B.G. Whoever does not hate or does not have any desire is the right *sannyāsi*, not the one who has taken *sannyāsa* and is thinking about worldly problems. Whoever one may be, there is no chance for inaction. Continued training of the mind has to be a constant occupation for right living. And chapter 5 of B.G. tells you that *sannyāsa* is not so easy. It is internal *sannyāsa*, by means of the attitude of actionlessness that is more difficult and which is what is wanted. That is why the *pancha-maha-yajña* has been prescribed as an atonement for all the different kinds of unethical things we may be making and for rightfully paying our gratitude to ancestors, to gods, to human beings and animals, to the needy and to guests. A grateful acceptance of everything as a Grace from the Supreme is a sine-qua-non. Enjoy the world, says *Īśopaniśad* but train yourself in *vairāgya* (dispassion). For nothing like *dhana* (wealth), *yauvana* (youth), etc. is permanent (Bhaja Govindam).

MYTH 3: '*Śraddhā* is considered to be blind faith'. Not at all. Our philosophy is not a belief-based system. There are five sense organs which tell us what and how things in the outer world work. *Śruti* (the *Vedas*) which is our sixth sense of knowledge tells us that there is something beyond the five senses. Can you say that you believe in only what you see? Are you really sure that the pilot of your air-flight has the necessary certificate of license, authority, etc. Don't you believe it without having to see it? Is that not Faith? There is a *subhaśita* which says (*daive tīrthe dvije mantre* ...) meaning: your response satisfaction from a devata, holy water, Brahmin priest, mantra, astrologer, physician, or guru, is commensurate with the type of faith/trust you have reposed in them Don't be a doubting Thomas!

MYTH 4: I am an intellectual; I can read myself and educate myself. This is again wrong. For you need a living guru, not to solve your worldly issues, but to show you your Self. It is he who charts *sādhanas* for you to make a self-transformation, to get mind purified (*citta-śuddhi*) and also to get a stability (*ekāgratā*) for the mind. It cannot be a casual effort. It has to be a continued life-long *sādhana* to transform all your *āsurī sampat* to a *daivī sampat.* The practical tip, for instance, to get *Titikṣā* (patience and forbearance) is to adopt the monthly fasting habit on, say, the Ekadashi day. Moderation in everything – movies, books, social media involvement – is a must. Ch.18 emphasizes *yajña*, *dāna* and tapas as the most fundamental requirement for self transformation. *Dāna* is not philanthropy; it is *dharma*. As far as the daily duties are concerned, the populist 'chalta hai' attitude is classified as a *tāmasi sampat* by the *Gītā*.

MYTH 5: We can ourselves understand Divinity in our own way. No. The divinity that is in every one of us as the Oneness of all beings and all creation, is not a thing to be inferred by mental gymnastics. *Vedas* and *Vedānta* have to educate you to tell you that chaos nearby and cosmos far away have a unity; it is all a *vibhuti* of the Supreme. You may not learn it by yourself. But if you follow *yogah karmasu kaushalam*, the Royal Path to the Oneness of the Universe will by itself open for you.

https://youtu.be/TGSzy0bU0cU

The Logic of Advaita Vedānta

Speaker: Swami Ishwarananda

Logic (*yukti*) cannot take us to *Brahman*. It is not dry logic that is used in *Advaita*. It has to be supported by *Śruti (*the *Vedas*). Śaṅkara adopts a method of thinking which is coordinated with the *śruti. Vedānta* teachers do have a great challenge to appease the student's questioning intellect and give appropriate answers. They have to make sure that the student does not stay totally at the intellectual level. *Na medhayā na bahudhā shrutena*, says the *Upaniṣad*. Make him think independently but not indifferently. *Yukti* is used more to discard the known untruth (like the absolute reality of the world) and go to the unknown *mithyātvam* of the world. *Mithyā* is not total unreality but it represents those that appear and either immediately or in due time disappear. The mirror image disappears in a short time. The world disappears in a certain amount of time.

But both have the disappearing (or non-existing) nature. So they are both *mithyā*.

Again *Advaita* does not start from zero level. There is already something known (much of them may be wrong according to *Advaita*). From this (wrongly) known things *Advaita* proceeds to unravel the unknown truths at higher levels. *Avidya* (Ignorance) does not mean a blank. It is mostly incomplete or incorrect knowledge. From this partial ignorance of the truth, *Advaita* takes you to the total truth. It is like the identification of a star through the branches of a nearby tree, then its branches, then a particular branch, then its leaves, then the tip of a twig, then the little space between two twigs and then see the star in the far far distant sky in that direction. Once you locate the star, neither the tree nor its branches have any significance. So logic is used in *Advaita* to take you to that level where you will yourself be able to understand that the Absolute Truth is beyond all logic. That is why *Upaniṣad* says: *'buddheh param'* and '*yato vāco nivartante*'.

Take the example of a child. Does the child learn from zero level? No. The child hears the sound, then words, sentences and then the meaning.

First it all starts from sound. The child has the ability to recognise the sound. So also all of us have a knowing ability through our intellect. This knowing bility is because of the reflection of Consciousness in our mind (*chidābhāsa*). This knowing ability is inherent in us. When we perceive an object and recognise it as an object, what has happened is: the reflected con-sciousness illuminates (to our mind) that object and that makes our mind 'perceive' it. It is the mind that goes (through its reflected consciousness) to the object and not the other way. This is what makes the mind an instrument of knowing. Remember during sleep we do not know anything; because the instrument of knowing, the mind, is not active. Only when the *antaḥkaraṇa* is present, can there be knowledge of anything. But Consciousness is always present and so is awareness of our sleep. Also when a man is preoccupied with something he does not even recognize the presence of a visitor. So then, who is the knower? It is the *Chidābhāsa*. So for knowing the highest truth this reflection of consciousness (in the 'mirror' of) our mind, must be pure. That is why all *Advaita* cries from the housetops that *chittaśuddhi (*purified mind) is an inescapable necessity. Mind is not endowed by itself to know; just as a bulb is not endowed with the power to illuminate, unless it has the electric power. So also the *Advaita*'s regimen is: Illuminated intellect (mind) by reflected consciousness sees (or thinks of) the object and illuminates it. But why does it differ from person to person? Because each person has a different quality of mind and so the *vrittis* that happen in the mind are different. This quality is a function of *samshaya* (doubt), *nishcaya* (exactness), *garva (*effect of ego) and *smarana* (memory). And so it differs from person to person and naturally the experience of the object also differs. So the *gunas* of *prakriti* are important. And Kṛṣṇa prescribes therefore '*nitya-satvastho bhava*'.

Now let us see how the logic is used in *Brahma-vicāra*. We don't begin by total ignorance. *Brahman* is partially known. How? Everybody says without any prompting: 'I AM'. All of us know 'I am'. 'I am what?' is the problem. Aham asmi — does not need any scholarship. '*aham brahma asmi*' has to be taught. So the individuality is there for everybody. But what the 'individual' is, is the subject of *Vedānta*. A sculptor looks at a rock. I also look at it. I see only the rock. But he sees '*Kṛṣṇa*' in it. How is it? I ask. He sculpts the *Kṛṣṇa* in it, and throws away the non-*Kṛṣṇa*. Now the *Kṛṣṇa* is recognisable also by me. So also the *ātman-brahman* which is what we are, is not recognisable by us until *Advaita-Vedānta*-sculptor shows it to us. That Sculptor is our Guru!

https://youtu.be/mhzP-y2t-y8

Valedictory Address by Swami Atmapriyananda

Swami ji recited two passages from *Taittirīyopaniṣad* (1-4-1 and 1-10-1) as a partial basis for his talk. These two passages are for a constant japa to awaken your *medhā* (intelligence and creativity). The whole aim of *Vedānta* is to make us all negate our innate habit of worldliness through the concepts of 'Me' and 'Mine'. It is the Ego which makes these concepts foremost in our mind. *Vedānta* says *drishhṭim jñānamayīm kritva brahma-māyāM pashyet* meaning, one's vision has to be through *jñāna* and to see the universe as nothing but *Brahman*. *Muṇḍakopaniśad* says (2-2-11): *Brahmaivedam amritam purastād* … etc. meaning, All this that is in front is *Brahman*, the immortal. *Brahman* is at the back, as also on the right and the left. It is extended above and below, too, the world is nothing but *Brahman*, the highest. *Advaita* is joy, not joyless. It does not take everything for granted. *Māṇḍūkya*

Upaniṣad revels in the unity of the individual with the universal. The *tripuṭi* of *jñātā* (knower) *jñāna* (knowledge) and *jñeyam* (to be known) – all three become one as the Ultimate Truth.

You can contact everything in the world. But can you contact yourself? Who is the 'Me' or 'I' who is constantly with us? He is the eye of the eyes, ear of the ear, soul of our soul, says *Kenopaniśad*. All these *Upaniṣads* were not composed as literature. They are Truths 'seen' by them as that which is nearer than the nearest! It is for this that our *medhā* has to be awakened. That is what the first passage of the *Taittirīyopaniṣad* chant that the Swami made in the beginning. It means: The Om that is preeminent in the *Vedas* that pervades all words. And that emerged from the immortal *Vedas* as their quintessence, may Om gratify me with intelligence (*medhā*).' The second passage chanted in the beginning (*aham vrikshasya reriva*...) is a victorious ecstatic declaration of one (Sage *Triṣanku*) who had tasted the Absolute Supreme. In *Brihadāraṇyakopaniṣad* there is an immortal conversation between husband and wife, *Yajñavalkya* and *Maitreyī*. I am leaving all this wealth to you, my dear wife, says *Yajñavalkya*, before he leaves to go to the forest as a *sannyāsi* in the enjoyment of the Supreme. The wife asks: What use is it to me if it cannot show me the Absolute Truth which you are after. This is a monumental record for *Sanātana Dharma*, because this unique conversation between husband and wife on *Brahman* is to be endeared in our heart as the bottomline teaching of all *Upaniṣads*. Once you are *ātmakāma*, desirous of the *ātman* and you realise it as an *āptakāma* (having obtained what you desired), you are then *akāma* (with no more desires). This is the *ātmasantushti* or *ātmarati* that the B.G. talks about. Sage Ramakrishna has put it all very succinctly in three short maxims: Continue asking *ko aham*? (Who am I). Keep feeling *nāham nāham* (I am not what I think I am, namely this BMI). And that will lead you to the final revelation '*so aham*', meaning I am He, the *Brahman*.

https://youtu.be/p8wMhjekJ0s

www.ingramcontent.com/pod-product-compliance
Lightning Source LLC
LaVergne TN
LVHW041147150826
845673LV00001B/88

* 9 7 9 8 8 9 1 3 3 4 4 2 7 *